how influence friends and tactfully get along with people

study of the book of Philemon

steve elzinga

How to Influence Friends and Tactfully Deal with People

By Steven Elzinga
Copyright ©2016 by the Christian Leaders Institute Publishing.

All rights reserved. No portion of this publication may be reproduced by any means without prior permission from the publisher: Christian Leaders Institute Publishing, PO Box 28000, Chicago IL 60628.

Holy Bible: Easy-to-Read Version™
Taken from the HOLY BIBLE: EASY-TO-READ VERSION™© 2006 by World Bible Translation Center, Inc. and used by permission.
THE HOLY BIBLE, NEW INTERNATIONAL VERSION®, NIV® Copyright © 1973, 1978, 1984, 2011 by Biblica, Inc.™ Used by permission. All rights reserved worldwide.

Scripture quotations marked (NLT) are taken from the Holy Bible, New Living Translation, Copyright © 1996, 2004, 2007 by Tyndale House Foundation. Used by permission of Tyndale House Publishers, Inc., Carol Stream, Illinois 60188. All rights reserved.

Why read this book/Bible study?

1. The hard part is already done - you started reading this book/Bible study.
2. This book/Bible study will give you more insights on how to deal with your relationships per square inch than any other book of its kind.
3. You will be able to immediately apply the principles found inside this book/Bible study to family, friends, your church community, workmates, clients, customers – any person with whom you have any kind of relationship.
4. Reading this book or doing it as a Bible study will help you interact with those around you with more confidence.
5. After reading this book/Bible study, you will be equipped with practical steps that will help you deal with difficult relationship situations.
6. As you read the pages of this small book/Bible study, you will be impressed with the wisdom of the Apostle Paul in this book of the Bible.
7. This book can be read like any book or it can be used like a Bible study.
8. There are five sermons that can be used as supplemental material for your personal enjoyment, or as a Bible study enhancement, or for a sermon series on Philemon at your church.

You will find these free sermons at www.path2jesusway.org

CLI Ministry Bible Studies

Use as a regular Bible study or with a small group or as a whole church Bible study and sermons series.

CLI Bible Study/Sermon Series

- *Genesis: The Foundation of Everything* (Books 1,2,3,4)
- *Acts: The Unbelievable Story of the Church*
- *Ephesians: Who are You?*
- *Daniel: Hope When Things Seem Hopeless*
- *The 7 Things Every Christian Should Know*
- *Lead Like Jesus*
- *Christmas Advent Bible Study*
- *7 Favorite Bible Stories that Kids Love*
- *Lifestyles of the Jesus Way*

Use as a regular Bible study or as a retreat theme.

CLI Bible Study/Retreat Series

- *Marriage Connection: Tips from a Guy Married 700 Times*
- *The Man-Up Bible Study*

Check out these & other ministry resources at
www.christianleadersinstitute.org/shop

CLI Bible Study/Book Series
- *Being a Lifeboat Church in a Titanic Cruiseship World*
- *Philemon: How to Win Friends and Tactfully Get Along with People*
- *The Secret of a Great Music Ministry Questions*
- *The Secret to a Great Preaching Ministry Questions*
- *The Secret to a Great Evangelism Ministry Questions*
- *The Jesus Bible Questions*
- *The 30 Second Bible*
- *Building a Walk-with-God Church*

Read as a book or use it as a Bible study.

CLI Walk-with-God Bible Studies
- *How to Get a Personal Walk with God*
- *How to Get a Marriage Walk with God*
- *How to Get a Family Walk with God*
- *How to Help Others Get a Walk with God*
- *How to Use Hospitality to Share Your Walk with God*
- *Being a Walk-with-God Church (The 7 Connections)*

This is one of the main themes at CLI.

Check out these & other ministry resources at www.christianleadersinstitute.org/shop

Table of Contents:

11	**Part One: The Back-Story**
29	**Part Two: The Relationship Principles**
	Step One: Relationship - Build it!
30	1. Communicate that you are friends
35	2. Communicate that you are both on the same side
43	3. Communicate that you both need God's grace
50	4. Communicate that you thank God for the other person
58	5. Communicate something positive about the other person
67	6. Communicate how blessed this person is
72	7. Communicate how much this person has done for you
	Step Two: Influence - Use it!
78	1. Appeal to a higher motive
85	2. Communicate your needs in the language of the other's needs
89	3. Appeal to mutual benefits
95	4. Share your heartfelt feelings in the matter

5. Suggest what you prefer, but leave the decision up to them	100
6. Communicate the potential good in the problem	105

Step Three: Commitment - Do it!

1. Make your request or suggestion with humility	110
2. Offer to help out where you can	115
3. Gently remind them of what they owe you	122
4. Expect the best	128
5. Ask for a lesser commitment you know they will succeed at	133
6. End your conversation talking about your common relationship web	139

Part Three: The Main Theme of the Book

The issue of slavery	145
End notes and questions	153

How this book/study works
Unique Options:

Option One: Use this book/study like any other book. Read each chapter and then use the questions to help you think about how what you read applies to your life.

Use as a book

Option Two: Use this book/study as a group Bible study. There are 19 lessons or chapters in the book. Each has a bit of reading and then six to eight questions that would help the group discuss what they read. The reading part could be done by each participant before the meeting or at the group meeting.

Use as a group Bible study

Option Three: Use any of the above options with the added component of the five **sermons** that go with this book. The first sermon is really just a live version of Part One. The next three sermons follow each of the three steps of Part Two. And the last sermon goes with Part Three. So the sermons can be used as added material to help participants with each of the five sections.

The sermon series can be found at www.path2jesusway.org

Option Four: Use the book as a sermon/Bible study for the whole church. This is how I did it:

Use as a Bible study supported sermon series

— *Sunday 1: Preach Part One*

　Mon - Sat: The congregation then did all seven lessons of Step One in their homes.

— *Sunday 2: Preach Part Two: Step One*

　Mon - Sat: The congregation then did all six lessons of Step Two in their homes.

— *Sunday 3: Preach Part Two: Step Two*

　Mon - Sat: The congregation then did all six lessons of Step Three in their homes.

— *Sunday 4: Preach Part Two: Step Three*

　Mon - Sat: The congregation then did the last lesson, Part Three, at some point in the week in their homes.

— *Sunday 5: Preach Part Three*

Check out these & other ministry resources at
www.christianleadersinstitute.org/shop

Note from the author of this Bible study:

As a Pastor, I slowly came to realize that many of the people attending my church were coming to the Worship service with great expectations of what I might be able to do for them. They wanted to be fed spiritual food that would give them hope and strength for whatever they would face in the week ahead. So I did my best to feed them. But I soon discovered that no matter how well I did on Sunday, it was not good enough to feed them for a week.

Has this thought ever occurred to you as well?

God gave me a new thought. **Why not teach them how to feed themselves?** Instead of the people showing up to church having done no work at all for the spiritual food they were about to partake in, why not get them working on the sermon with me - all week long?

So I developed Bible Studies like this one on the book of Philemon from the Bible. The whole church studies the topic of the week and Bible passages that support that topic every day in their personal lives, their marriages and in their families. All of this is then reinforced and expanded on in small groups. And finally, the whole process culminates in the church service where the pastor gets to preach a powerful message that everyone has been involved with all week long.

In my church, this approach has transformed my bench sitters into players, my attenders to activists, and my critical back seat drivers to encouraging front seat supporters.

Steve Elzinga
Pastor at Pathway Church &
Professor at CLI

Part One: The Back-Story

Philemon

We had no idea that he was coming until the knock on the door. How he dared to come back at all was beyond me. At first, I didn't see him because he was standing behind the man who had escorted him to my house. This man I knew. His name was Tychicus. He was a good friend of **Epaphras** who was a student of the great Apostle Paul. It was Epaphras that exposed me to the new religion called "Christianity." As Tychicus introduced himself to me, I finally noticed the man standing behind him. It was Onesimus, my runaway slave.

I had expected that the next time I would see him he would be in chains. But here he

---

Paul writes about Epaphras in his letter to the Colossians:

"Epaphras, who is one of you and a servant of Christ Jesus, sends was, unbound, and dressed as any free man.

He said nothing, hiding behind his escort. I said nothing as well, patiently letting Tychicus explain how the two of them had traveled several weeks from the capital city of Rome. As he recounted their journey, I carefully observed Onesimus. He was thin, but he had always been thin. His eyes flitted back and forth - not focusing on anything in particular. His hands were behind his back as if in shackles, though they were not. He rocked, hesitantly, back and forth. You could tell he was nervous. As well he should be.

I felt a resentment rising to anger within me. He deserved the death penalty. That would be justice for his crime.

Tychicus finally broke the tension in this unlikely turn of events. He reached out his hand - and in his hand was a letter - a letter apparently written by the Apostle Paul.

My name is Philemon. I grew up in the once thriving city of **Colossi,** built on an important east-west trade route leading from the Aegean seaport of Ephesus to the Euphrates River, which brought goods all the way to Babylon. But that was 200 years ago. Now Laodicea and its neighboring city Hierapolis, with its healing hot springs, dominate the area.

Though from Colossi, I spent most of my

---

greetings." He is always wrestling in prayer for you, that you may stand firm in all the will of God, mature and fully assured. 13 I vouch for him that he is working hard for you and for those at Laodicea and Hierapolis." (Colossians 4:12-13)

Colossi is the city that lends its name to the letter Paul writes called Colossians.

The Back Story

life away from it as a Roman Commander. I lived wherever Rome sent me.

As a military man, I had but two allegiances - the Emperor and the soldiers I commanded. The former called himself a god, but no one believed that. If he were a god, then he would have to get in line with all the other gods that people felt an obligation to honor. It seemed each city had one. I never found the gods of any particular use. But I honored them just the same, as did everybody else. What harm could there be?

> *Like many of us today!*

I **busied** myself with doing my job and doing it better than anyone else. I had no time or inclination to worry about anything else.

But then my job ended. I moved to my hometown of Colossi to be with my wife and our grown children and began to live what I thought would be the good life.

But what was good about my new life? I had no men to lead. I had no emperor to follow. What was I to do? What was my purpose? What was the meaning of life and death?

When a soldier, I never worried about dying. If I died, it was for the cause, it was for the Emperor, it was for my men. I felt there would be some kind of glory in it - among men and the gods. But now I had nothing to die for and, I soon realized, nothing to live for either.

My mind would turn these thoughts over and over. I became anxious.

So for the first time in my life, I studied my options.

The Roman gods held little meaning to me. So I turned to philosophy. Not really a religion per se, but, at least philosophers were trying to find answers to the questions that I had. What is true? What is real? What is life about? Where is it all going?

Of the many philosophies of the day, two were the most popular: Stoicism and Epicureanism.

According to the **Stoic**, life is determined. All the particles and material of this world are following a predetermined pattern. So what is going to happen is going to happen. Worrying is pointless.

Since all of life is determined, there is a certain logic to it all. Finding out what that logic is would be how one should spend his time.

And somehow, being good and doing good are the ways to happiness. But happiness, according to the Stoic, is not an emotion. Emotions are distractions, false realities. The pursuit of goodness and reason and logic is what life is about for a Stoic.

I had many Stoic friends who did a lot of good and never seemed to be bothered by the negative circumstances of their lives.

> A Stoic, was one who followed Stoicism, a school of Hellenistic philosophy founded in Athens by Zeno of Citium in the early 3rd century BC.

The Back Story

Epicureanism is a system of philosophy based upon the teachings of the ancient Greek philosopher Epicurus, founded around 307 BC.

They seemed content and strong. And they, unlike me, slept like babies.

But, and this is what soured me on this philosophy, if all the material of this world is following a particular predetermined pattern, where did that pattern come from or from whom and to what purpose?

So I turned to the other great philosophy, **Epicureanism.**

If Stoics shunned the material world, Epicureans embraced it. Life, to their way of thinking, was first and foremost about pleasure - one's own pleasure.

At first, I thought this was a young man's philosophy - you have to be young to take advantage of it. But, as my friends following this philosophy explained, pleasure only comes to those who limit their wants. Too much of a good thing is not always good. In fact, most things in life are better, more enjoyable, the harder they are to come by or the longer we have to wait for them.

I thought I had found the answer - to live a simple life and to enjoy simple pleasures, all the while achieving tranquility.

But my new philosophy did not quiet my troubled mind in the end. I found no purpose in pursuing my pleasures. It just didn't work. I got bored with myself. My little life, as it happens, was, I am afraid to say, not purposeful enough.

That is when a friend of mine introduced me to a friend of his, Epaphras, who was a disciple of the Apostle Paul, the great missionary of a new religion called Christianity. He tried to tell me about this new religion, and at first, I laughed it off. Why would anyone be crazy enough to adopt a religion that worshiped a man we Romans had killed on a cross?

But one night, I listened to what Epaphras had to say. He explained how the foundation of the Christian faith was Judaism. At this, I laughed out loud and told him he was making his views harder for me to believe. But I listened, and I was intrigued.

Unlike the Roman pantheon of many gods seemingly chosen for political reasons, Judaism had only one God. And He supposedly created everything out of nothing. This God could not be made into an image of gold or silver by a man, but men and women were made and shaped by Him.

Epaphras explained to me about Adam and Eve and the garden of paradise that God had provided them. He told how sin came into the world through a lie spoken by a fallen angel - a lie that promised that mere men and women could become gods. Of course, this is what we Romans believed - that mere men and women could become gods.

When Epaphras described how Adam and Eve believed the lie and then, as a result, felt the need to hide, not only from each other in their newly discovered nakedness, but also from their God, I felt convicted. I had been hiding behind my uniform most of my life. I had been hiding behind the importance that I felt when people did what I said. I had been hiding behind my wealth that allowed me to control the people around me. I had been hiding behind the connection I had to the Emperor of Rome - a so-called god.

What are some of the lies you have been hiding behind?

All of it was a lie. All of it was a cover up for an insecure man trying desperately to be significant, to be somebody.

This lie, a lie I could not hide from anymore, caused me great shame.

So, I listened with real interest when Epaphras told of God's plan to bring His prized creation, the men and women that He loved, out of insecurity, smallness, shame, and even death itself. God, he explained to me, had chosen a simple man named **Abraham**. And he did so with these words, "I will make you into a great nation, and I will bless you; I will make your name great, and you will be a blessing ... and all peoples on earth will be blessed through you."

See Genesis 12

Abraham passed this promise on to his son Isaac, and then Isaac passed it on to his son Jacob, who had 12 sons. Jacob's descendants eventually became the 12 tribes of Israel.

Though the promise was passed down to

the descendants of Jacob, they ended up as slaves in Egypt.

"But," explained Epaphras, "God heard the cries of his people in slavery, and he sent a savior named Moses to lead the people out of slavery - out of hiddenness, guilt, and shame."

As he talked about this part of his story, I wondered about my slaves. Were they praying for deliverance?

Then Epaphras told me about Jesus - the Son of God, who died at the hands of Roman soldiers like me. "But He died," Epaphras said looking me straight in the eye, "to take your place, to take on your guilt so that you can come out from hiding, insecurity, and shame."

And then Epaphras said something so ridiculous that I almost choked on the piece of bread I was eating. "Jesus died at the hands of Roman soldiers like you, Philemon, but three days later he was resurrected. He walked among us. He then commissioned us to tell others about Him. Then He left for His Kingdom in Heaven. He is there preparing for our arrival when we die."

Epaphras then challenged me to live my life as a Christian - a follower of Christ.

And when I asked what a follower of Christ was, he said, "One who believes in Christ, lives for Christ, and shares Christ with oth-

The Back Story

Philemon 1:1-3 (NIV) Paul, a prisoner of Christ Jesus, and Timothy our brother, To Philemon our dear friend and fellow worker—also to Apphia our sister and Archippus our fellow soldier—and to the church that meets in your home: Grace and peace to you from God our Father and the Lord Jesus Christ.

ers."

I did believe. And I began to tell others. And with the help of Epaphras, I started a **church in my home**. It changed my life. I finally had something to believe in that gave me real purpose and meaning to my life.

But something was missing. I believed it, and I was sharing it, but was I living it?

I felt like I was still hiding behind the image I had carefully fashioned all my life. I was still wealthy and powerful. I still liked these things. I had become a Christian, but I wasn't sure how to apply my Christianity to the people around me.

One sign of my power and wealth were my slaves. I once managed soldiers that I paid a wage. Now I controlled slaves that I owned. Owning slaves was quite common in the Roman world. You conquer nations; they become your slaves. Slaves do what you want them to do. They serve you. They have no choice in the matter. They exist to please you.

I considered myself a good master before becoming a Christian - especially to my most useful slave, Onesimus. I treated him like a son. I let him manage many of my affairs. I even trusted him with money transactions. I cared for him, and he lacked for nothing.

After I had become a Christian, I admit I did not share my newfound faith with my slaves.

Slaves are slaves. They have no rights. The master's religion is the master's religion. Slaves must find their religion. But, having said that, I was a good provider.

So, you can understand, perhaps, my bewilderment when I found Tychicus and Onesimus standing at my door with a letter from the Apostle Paul. What could this be?

Onesimus:

I had to leave. I was not born a slave. And when I left, I never thought I would come back - at least not of my choosing.

Some 20 years ago, the mighty Roman Empire, as it expanded to the far corners of the earth, finally had arrived with its legions of soldiers at my little corner of the earth.

My people, a fierce, proud tribe in northern **Britannia**, foolishly resisted and inevitably paid a high price for their pride. Death. Rape. Slavery.

At the time, I thanked the gods of my tribe that I only had to pay the price with slavery. The rest of my family paid with their lives.

I was ten years old. My gods, my family, my homeland - all that communicated a person's worth - gone.

I now had to forge meaning from a new reality. Slavery. My new god was my master, and my value as a human being was depen-

Present day Great Britain.

dent on his need of me. I had to be useful.

I learned to serve my master. As I grew into manhood, I became his most valuable slave. Whatever was needed, I could make happen.

That is how I got my name, "Onesimus," which means "useful." I was useful. My life depended on it.

Being useful was enough at first. I would have stayed a slave, content in being useful to my master, but then my master became a follower of **the Way**. He became a Christian. Soon many of my master's friends did the same. They began to meet in our house. Slaves were not welcome at these meetings. Over time, however, I learned about the Way. And I have to confess, I was intrigued.

I learned that the God of this new Way had chosen a people long ago, but that these people had become slaves like me. God then heard their cry for help and sent a savior named Moses to lead them to freedom.

I learned from some letters read in meetings in our home, letters written by some teacher of the Way named Paul, that all men are born slaves and must be freed by what Jesus did on the cross.

I didn't understand the whole thing, but the desire for freedom and the hope that it was possible was born in me.

But nothing came of it. Lives were being

The WAY became another name for Christianity.

Acts 9:1-2
Saul ... went to the high priest and asked him for letters to the synagogues in Damascus, so that if he found any there who belonged to the Way ...

changed, supposedly, in the church in our house, but my life as a slave stayed the same.

I could no longer get my value from just being useful to my master Philemon. The **possibility of hope** created such a desire in me that I had to do something.

I decided to escape. Having been the right-hand man of my master for so many years, I was familiar with travel, history, accounts, maps, and the ways of the world.

I decided to make my way to Rome - a place of opportunity, a place of obscurity, a place to hide, a place to make my way.

The journey to Rome was not without adventure. I made it. Upon arrival, I joined in with all the other misfits and foreigners seeking to find a better way.

My skills at being useful to people helped me, not only to survive in this chaotic and strange new city, but also, ultimately, to thrive.

But no matter how successful I became, I always slept with one eye open. One slip of the tongue, one misstep and I could be exposed for the liar that I was. And, if that were to happen, death.

One day, as I was doing business in the market, a most astounding thing happened. I heard two people talking about the Way. Was it the same Way of my former mas-

Where has this happened in your life?

ter Philemon? I listened to them. I followed them. They led me to a house. It turned out to be the prison house of the Apostle Paul - the one I had heard about at the estate of my former master Philemon.

Over the next several months, I became useful to the Apostle Paul. But as I served him, I made it clear to him that he was not my master, and I was not his slave.

He responded in, what I soon learned all too well, **classic Paul**. He said to me, "All men are slaves to whatever they serve, whether power, riches, popularity, glory, or God. The only freedom one has is in choosing what or whom one serves."

So, apparently, I had escaped one master only to end up serving another. I could leave at any time, but in the end, I had to serve something or someone. At the moment of leaving one master to serve another, I would become a slave again. Slavery is inevitable. So freedom is really about choosing one's slavery wisely.

I decided to enslave myself to a God that loved me so much that He sent His only Son to die to set me free from sin and death.

I became a follower of Christ and the Way. And my life was filled with meaning and purpose as I attended to the needs of perhaps the most influential Christian alive.

But I was hiding something. My past.

Romans 6:17-18 (NIV)
But thanks be to God that, though you used to be slaves to sin, you have come to obey from your heart the pattern of teaching that has now claimed your allegiance. You have been set free from sin and have become slaves to righteousness.

One night, as I was attending to his needs, the Apostle Paul said, with a mischievous smile on his face, something about being a prisoner - not only of the Romans but also of Christ. He said it like it was a good thing. That is when I knew I had to tell him the truth about who I was.

Of course, he somehow knew already, but he was waiting for me to be ready. We talked all night. In the morning, he looked me in the eye and asked me what I thought I should do.

I knew what he wanted me to say, but I couldn't. How could Paul know what **Philemon** would do if I went back? Philemon had treated me, in some ways, like a son - mentoring me, giving me responsibility, trusting me with everything as his most trusted slave. And how did I reward my master for everything he had done for me? Betrayal.

How would I be able to explain that I was thankful for all I had been given, but I did not want to be treated as a slave or even as a surrogate son? I wanted to be treated as a brother ... a brother in Christ.

Paul must have known what I was thinking and finally said, "Let me write a letter to Philemon explaining things. I will let you read it. If you like it, we can send it. If not, we won't. What do you say?"

This is the letter both Tychicus and I brought to the house of Philemon:

> Philemon could legally have Onesimus killed for his betrayal.

The Apostle Paul:

Philemon 1:1-2 Paul, a prisoner of Christ Jesus, and Timothy our brother, to Philemon our dear friend and fellow worker — also to Apphia our sister and Archippus our fellow soldier — and to the church that meets in your home:

3 Grace and peace to you from God our Father and the Lord Jesus Christ. 4-5 I always thank my God as I remember you in my prayers, because I hear about your love for all his holy people and your faith in the Lord Jesus.

6 I pray that the faith you share will make you understand every blessing we have in Christ.

7 Your love has given me great joy and encouragement, because you, brother, have refreshed the hearts of the Lord's people.

8-9a Therefore, although in Christ I could be bold and order you to do what you ought to do, yet I prefer to appeal to you on the basis of love.

9b-10 It is as none other than Paul—an old man and now also a prisoner of Christ Jesus— that I appeal to you for my son Onesimus, who became my son while I was in chains.

11 Formerly he was useless to you, but now he has become useful both to you and to me.

These first five verses are from the New International Version of the Bible.

Verses 6 and 7 are from the Easy to Read Version of the Bible.

Verse 8 to the end of the book of Philemon is from the New International Version of the Bible.

12 I am sending him—who is my very heart—back to you.

13-14 I considered keeping him with me so that he might serve me in your place during my time in prison because of the gospel. However, I didn't want to do anything without your consent so that your act of kindness would occur willingly and not under pressure.

15-16 Maybe this is the reason that Onesimus was separated from you for a while so that you might have him back forever— no longer as a slave but more than a slave—that is, as a dearly loved brother. He is especially a dearly loved brother to me. How much more can he become a brother to you, personally and spiritually in the Lord!

17 So if you consider me a partner, welcome him as you would welcome me. 18 If he has done you any wrong or owes you anything, charge it to me.

19 I, Paul, am writing this with my own hand. I will pay it back—not to mention that you owe me your very self.

20 I do wish, brother, that I may have some benefit from you in the Lord; refresh my heart in Christ. 21 Confident of your obedience, I write to you, knowing that you will do even more than I ask.

22 And one thing more: Prepare a guest

room for me, because I hope to be restored to you in answer to your prayers.

23 Epaphras, my fellow prisoner in Christ Jesus, sends you greetings. 24 And so do Mark, Aristarchus, Demas and Luke, my fellow workers.

25 The grace of the Lord Jesus Christ be with your spirit.

Part Two: The Principles

STEP ONE: Relationship - Build it.

1. Communicate that you are friends.

There is nothing more powerful in building a relationship than calling someone "my friend."

And yet these words are rarely used.

Why?

Most of us do not have very many **friends**. Perhaps we made a few friends in our school days. But many of those friendships have dissolved with the passing of time and places. We make friends in our workplaces, but when jobs change and transfers are had, these friendships also don't last long.

I read somewhere that for the average man his spouse is his best friend. With so many

Philemon 1:1 Paul, a prisoner of Christ Jesus, and Timothy our brother, to Philemon our dear friend...

Whom do you consider your friends?

marriages ending in divorce, this fact seems somewhat depressing.

But why does it have to be this way? Why don't we make friends with a lot of people? Not everyone is going to be your best friend or maybe even a close friend, but why can't lots and lots of people receive the label "friend"?

Perhaps the problem is we have too high of a standard for the label "friend."

We think, perhaps idealistically, that friends should have a lot in common and do a lot of things together. Friends should have a long history. Friends should be few, exclusive, and rare.

Some people secretly feel that friendship should be an "understood" thing between people, and that the words "you are my friend" should not be spoken.

But why should we be so limiting with the "friend" status or the friend label for that matter?

What if the only criteria for friendship was the desire to bless someone?

"I am interested in your well-being as well as my own. And sometimes I must sacrifice to help you out and sometimes you must sacrifice to help me out. And often doing things together is a blessing for both of us."

Paul writes to Philemon and, in the first sentence, calls him a beloved friend.

Step One: Relationship - Build it!

The issue of the status of Onesimus.

What is Paul communicating to Philemon by calling him a friend?

1. That the **issue** they are about to discuss is between friends.
2. That they are not enemies where one is against the other.
3. That they are not competitors where one wins and the other loses.
4. That as friends each should have a desire for outcomes that benefit both.
5. That both, to some degree, should be willing to sacrifice his rights for a greater good.

Are these not good things to communicate to a person with whom you are about to have a delicate and challenging discussion?

"Okay," you may be wondering, "but isn't calling someone a friend for the purpose of gaining some advantage in a negotiation or issue manipulation?"

Yes, it can be. But there is another side to calling someone friend. If I call you friend, not only will you be more inclined to listen, negotiate, compromise, and even, perhaps, give in to my point of view, but - and here is the point - I will be more inclined to do the same for you.

If friendship is a one-way street, then it is not a friendship relationship. It is a dependent relationship.

Friendship is a two-way street. I help you. You help me. I pay for the dinner at the restaurant one time, and you get it the next.

So why not try expanding the borders of those you call a friend? Pick out someone who is not that close to you, and find an excuse to call him your friend.

How? Shake this person's hand the next time you meet him or her, and say, "It is great to see you, my friend." Or do it in an email: "Hey, friend, let's do lunch this week." Don't make a big deal about it, but **do it**.

Then stay in contact with this person for a couple of weeks and see what happens to the relationship.

Try it on your boss. A coworker. Someone at church that serves on the same committee that you do.

Why not even try it on your spouse? If your spouse has never heard you use the word "friend" to describe your relationship, try it. You will see a difference in your relationship.

Next, try it with your kids, the neighbor next door, and even the mail carrier.

If you want to see change in your relationships, you can't just read this book. You have to put what you read into practice.

Questions:

1. Why do you think Paul starts his letter to Philemon calling him "a dear friend" or more literally, "dearly beloved"?

2. Why do you think that people do not often call each other friend?

3. When in your life have people you considered your friends come through for you? What did they do?

Step One: Relationship - Build it!

4. If you were to call someone a friend, what would that mean?

5. Why is it sometimes difficult to make and maintain a friendship?

6. What sometimes makes solving a problem harder to do among friends?

7. What advantage do friends have in solving a problem that arises between them?

STEP ONE: Relationship - Build it.
2. Communicate that you are both on the same side.

If you have a relationship issue (an issue that puts you on opposite sides) with someone, it is usually with someone close to you. I mean, who cares if someone you hardly know has an issue with you?

The relationship issues we tend to lose sleep over are the ones we have with people that we know well, the people we do things with on a consistent basis, the people that are on our team, the people that are, supposedly, on our side.

Like who?

> Philemon 1:2
> ... and fellow worker— also to Apphia our sister and Archippus our fellow soldier—and to the church that meets in your home:

Step One Relationship: Build it!

Your spouse. Your son. Your daughter. The people at work. Your neighbors and friends. The people at church. The guy with whom you do business. Your father or mother. Your brother or sister. Anyone that you know.

Like what issues?

Betrayal. Your spouse cuts you down consistently, not so much to your face or even behind your back, but in front of your friends. Your friends become the judge and jury before which your marriage trial takes place. You have communicated your disapproval of this behavior to your spouse, but that just starts a complaining match.

What would happen if you did not retaliate in kind to your spouse's public insults, but instead, began to consistently, in a winning, courteous, enthusiastic manner, communicate the positives of being on the same **team**?

Gossip. You know there is something wrong when the people in your life start avoiding you. Someone has been saying things, negative things, about you. When you find out what is being said and by whom, what will you do?

When I find out that someone has been gossiping about me, my instinct is to pick up the phone or drive over to the perpetrator's house and ask him or her what in the world is going on. That usually does not go well.

We sometimes say negative things about people behind their back because we are too insecure to say it to their face.

> *I often use the words, "Team Steve and Marie" when talking about my marriage and the things we are doing.*
>
> *Matthew 18:15-20. Following the outline of Matthew 18 is a great way to avoid gossiping about others.*

Competition. I completed my seminary training, and a church wanted me to be their pastor. I was ready. I was confident. I was eager to get on with ministry. Some of the church people helped my wife and I move our one van load of stuff into the **parsonage**. My books went into the pastor's study at church.

> The church house.

One of my new parishioners stopped by to meet the new pastor. After introducing himself to me, he paused to look at my books. After giving them the once over, he looked at me and said, "I have more books than you."

Turns out his family was one of the most influential families in the history of that area. He had thought about going to seminary as a young man but instead became a wealthy farmer.

For the next four years, it was game on. Both he and I competed as if we were on opposing teams. When I preached, he would not look at me. In fact, he would sit sideways facing the wall.

It was a great church, but that one relationship was a constant drag on my enthusiasm for ministry.

What could I have done differently?

I could have, in one way or another, communicated that both he and I, despite our differences, despite our likes and dislikes, notwithstanding the number of books either of us had, regardless of talent or lack thereof, are on the same side.

Step One: Relationship - Build it!

Let's expand this. What would happen if you routinely and consistently communicated to your problem teenager, to the lazy guy at work, to your nagging spouse, to that person at work who is always taking sides against you that ...

"We are on the same side!"

By the way, the guy that was a thorn in my side in my first church wrote me a letter many years later. He apologized.

Disagreements. It had been another late board meeting at the church. A proposal to add a morning service that was more contemporary and "seeker-sensitive" was put before the congregation and it passed. That was 1986, and I had never heard of churches doing this before.

But now those that disagreed with the change that the proposal entailed came out in force to protect their interests.

The issue was not just the addition of another service, but a change of time for the current morning service - a half an hour change. If you want to hear church people whine and cry, try changing the service time.

The board was meeting, and folks had arrived to voice their objections - even though everyone already had a chance to speak up when the vote was taken. Some were just not going to accept "yes" for an answer.

Woman: Why are we doing this?

Pastor: Our church is full; we need to do

something.

Woman: We could squeeze a few more people in the front next to the pulpit.

Pastor: New people come late; they will not sit up front in front of everyone.

Woman: Well, why don't they come on time like we do?

Pastor: I don't know. That's just the way it is. I'm just glad they are coming at all.

Woman: Well, if they want our benefits, they will have to sacrifice for them.

Pastor: They, the newcomers, should do the sacrificing?

Woman: That's the question, isn't it? Who should do the sacrificing, us or them? After all, we built the church; we paid for it.

This is where I wanted to scream and say, "If God had that kind of attitude, where would you and I be? He **sacrificed** His only Son for us. We are the ones who are called to pick up our cross daily and follow Him."

Was I wrong? No, my logic was sound. My answers were Biblical. But what did this woman hear? She heard that this disagreement put us on opposite sides.

There are two steps in an argument.

Step one is - I disagree with you.

John 3:16 (NIV) For God so loved the world that he gave his one and only Son, that whoever believes in him shall not perish but have eternal life.

Step two is - I tell you that I do not agree with you.

It takes a lot of energy to go from step one to step two. Usually, it is negative energy.

People, when they feel the need to confront or oppose something, are not ready for a logical defense. They need to unload a shotgun full of negative emotion. They want you to listen. You or somebody stepped on their feelings. They are full of righteous indignation. They have rehearsed their response to the situation over and over in their minds. They have burdened close friends with their concern. They have lost sleep. And in the end, they see you as one who is on the "other side."

When people do this to me, I want to correct their thinking and, despite my experience to the contrary, I often think that I can clear things up in a sentence or two. But tankers do not turn on a dime. Neither do people in a disagreement.

Most people start from the perception that the other guy is wrong and they are right.

Since disagreements put people on opposite sides, the first thing you need to do to resolve the conflict is establish that you and the one you have a disagreement with, though you may disagree with each other, are not on opposite sides.

So how in the world do you communicate, in the middle of a dispute or disagreement, that you are both, in fact, on the same side?

Talk about **past events** - occasions where you were literally on the same side of some issue that was a threat to the both of you.

Talk about current issues that you know that you both agree on.

Communicate in some way: "We are both followers of Christ. We both want to walk with God in our personal lives and marriages and families, and we want to share that walk with others. We are members of the **one body of Christ**, and we belong to each other."

i.e. I might say to my wife, "Remember when we got lost and we had to ...."

Romans 12:5 (NLT) We are many parts of one body, and we all belong to each other.

Questions:

1. Why do teammates, co-workers, partners, and even fellow church members sometimes fight amongst each other?

    1 Corinthians 11:18 In the first place, I hear that when you come together as a church, there are divisions among you ...

2. Why does conflict with friends, family, co-workers, and even church members often cause hard feelings?

3. Why do you think people are often threatened by individuals on their team?

Step One: Relationship - Build it!

4. How does the following verse set out the proper perspective on how teammates should see each other?

   1 Corinthians 3:8-9 The one who plants and the one who waters have one purpose, and they will each be rewarded according to their labor. For we are co-workers in God's service; you are God's field, God's building.

5. Which relationship issue mentioned in this chapter can you relate to the most (betrayal, gossip, competition, or disagreement) and why?

6. Instead of escalating the relationship issue you might have with someone, how might you instead communicate that you are on the same team?

7. What do you think are the quality characteristics of a team member?

8. Whom can you reassure that they are an important part of the team?

STEP ONE: Relationship - Build it.

3. Communicate that you both need God's grace.

Paul offers grace and peace to Philemon from God the Father and the Lord Jesus Christ. Why does he do this?

Today, we greet people with, "How are you?" We don't mean anything by it. It is just a greeting. So, maybe offering grace to someone back then was just a greeting.

Or maybe Paul was indeed offering the grace and peace of God the Father and the Lord Jesus Christ to Philemon.

> Philemon 1:3
> Grace and peace to you from God our Father and the Lord Jesus Christ.

Step One: Relationship - Build it!

How important is being right to you?

My dad, like many dads, was always right. At least, that is what I thought that he thought. And, if he was always right, then I was always wrong. I did not like being wrong. Not only did I not like being wrong (even when I was wrong), but I knew that sometimes I was not wrong. I was right sometimes. In fact, **I was more often right than wrong**. At least, that is how I felt.

Well, who doesn't feel this way?

In a church where I was the pastor, a member was not happy with me. When I visited him, he said, among other nasty things, that my sermons weren't Biblical.

I asked for a few examples so I could better understand what he was talking about, and he told me he couldn't be expected to remember examples.

So I then asked him to consider last Sunday's sermon, did he remember that?

He did remember it, and he thought it wasn't very Biblical.

I asked what part of my explanation of the Prodigal Son (that was my sermon on Luke 15) was un-Biblical.

He said that the whole thing was un-Biblical.

I then responded with, "If the whole thing was un-Biblical, then it shouldn't be hard to give me an example of one thing that I said that was un-Biblical."

He just repeated that the whole thing was un-Biblical.

I then asked how he could expect to convince me that he was right if he couldn't give me one example.

His response, "You are **arrogant**."

I had been patient up to this point, but now, having been unfairly insulted, I unsheathed my logic sword. Looking back, this was probably not the right thing to do to fix our broken relationship, but in the heat of the battle, it did produce a moment of insightful clarity (of course, I say this as only my humble opinion). I looked him in the eye and asked, "Can I ask you a question? Who is more arrogant? Is it the one being called arrogant or the one doing the calling?"

Who have you called or at least thought of as arrogant?

He said nothing. So I continued.

"You call me arrogant, and maybe that is so. But aren't you just as arrogant or perhaps even more so than me as you stand on some self-righteous mountain and look down on me. You appoint yourself the judge and jury in my case, you deliver your sentence on me without a trial of any sort, and then you refuse to tell me any of the grounds upon which you judge me."

He said nothing. He learned nothing. I learned nothing. And a friendship of five years came to an end.

But I was right, right? I mean, he was arrogant to call me arrogant? Right? That is my insight.

But, if **being right** is what is important in your

What are you adamantly right about these days?

relationship with someone, then you will always have a fight on your hands.

I don't care how wrong a person may be. No one, let me repeat that, no one wants anyone telling them that they are wrong.

I am not saying it is impossible for a person to admit they are wrong. It is more than possible. It is necessary if one wants success in any relationship. What I am saying is that it is very difficult to admit one is wrong when others are trying to force it on you.

So why do we do it? Why do we have this need to correct, rebuke, and criticize our spouses, family members, co-workers, pastors, and fellow church members?

There may be many reasons, but let me tell you the biggest. People have corrected, rebuked, and criticized us!

It starts with our parents. We grow up and go to school, and teachers share the load. Add to this a few coaches and finish it off with a few bosses.

Correction, rebuke, and criticism are all around us, and for the most part, it is productive - it brings the best out of us.

But in these cases, generally, it is expected or a part of an unspoken deal we have with teachers and mentors. When a kid signs up for a baseball team, he is in effect saying to the coach, "I understand that when I sign up for this team, it not only means that I am giving consent, but I am also asking for your correction, rebuke, and criticism. I understand that the motivation for all of this will be for my enrichment."

So we are ready for it. We know that criticism is coming and is given because someone cares for us and wants the best for us.

But when, for example, someone criticizes you for something you have done or not done and that same person has never encouraged you or said anything positive to you in your past, it comes off hurtful.

People do it to you; so you do it to others.

Paul, right away in his opening salutation to Philemon, affirms the need for grace and peace.

Grace assumes that both you and I are not perfect. Grace assumes that neither one of us is likely to be 100% right. Which means, in all likelihood, both of us could be wrong.

What does grace do for two people about to deal with a difficult relationship issue? It gives each of them the **freedom to be wrong**.

What does the freedom to be wrong do for a person? It frees them to truly look at the issue at hand with an open and humble mind.

"I don't have to be right. If I am wrong, I am loved by God no less. I am still a child of the King. In fact, Jesus died on the cross to pay for all my wrongness. I don't have to hide it or defend it."

So maybe Paul's words, "Grace to you and peace from God the Father and the Lord Je-

This might be worth writing down.

sus Christ," were more than a greeting. Maybe these words were a necessary ingredient in solving a relationship issue.

So why not **try this greeting out** for a week or two. Offer these words to your spouse first thing in the morning. Then to your kids at breakfast. How about to the people at work or school? At first, it may seem awkward. But soon people will know you for this greeting.

Of course, if this is going to be your greeting you will have to start living it.

How?

By giving yourself and the people around you the grace to be wrong.

Again, your relationships will not improve just because you read this book. Do something.

Questions:

> *Ephesians 2:8-10 For it is by grace you have been saved, through faith--and this is not from yourselves, it is the gift of God-- not by works, so that no one can boast. For we are God's handiwork, created in Christ Jesus to do good works, which God prepared in advance for us to do.*

1. In an argument, both parties tend to think they are right and, therefore, often do not listen to the other side. How is this like boasting?

2. Why do you think most people have a great need to be right?

3. Why would the need to be right be a burden?

4. Why would the ability to face the possibility of being wrong be freeing?

5. Into what troubling relationship do you need to interject a little grace?

6. Before two Christians talk about some difficult or sensitive issue where there may be some hurt feelings, why would acknowledging God's grace be a good way to start a conversation?

STEP ONE: Relationship - Build it.

4. Communicate that you thank God for the other person.

> Philemon 1:4
> I always thank my God as I remember you in my prayers ...

Don't you just hate it when someone comes up to you and says:

"Do you have a minute?"

"I have some concerns."

"I would like to talk to you."

"Can I speak candidly with you?"

"I have heard several people say some things, and I would like to talk to you about it."

You know what is coming. This friend, acquaintance, teacher, or boss wants to set you straight on something, and they have already judged you guilty and in need of their critique.

A few years ago, I had the whole prayer team from the church that had just called me to be their pastor come up to me with this kind of thing.

"Pastor, a few of us concerned members want you to know that we have been praying for you over these last few months. And we have gathered up our concerns and have assembled them into this anonymous letter we would like you to read."

When people tell you that they have been praying for you, it is not always a good thing.

I had pastored two churches before. This was my third - a then struggling, once thriving church that was imploding in on itself. I had succeeded in my first church - a country church that doubled in size. I had succeeded in my second church - a church plant in Vancouver, Canada, that had daughtered two churches. But this, my third church, was another story.

Though once a congregation of 300 people, it had dwindled down to 100 or so. The previous pastor received most of the blame for the downturn and was let go. With a lot of hope and promise, I was called to take his place.

Good things had happened in my previous churches. But not with this one. Under my expert leadership, I helped lead this church from 100 people down to 50.

So, I suppose there were plenty of things to pray about for this group of concerned members.

Back to the letter; I refused to take it or read

it. I have always refused to read anonymous letters. My feeling is that if you have something to say or write, attach your name to it or forget about it.

The group was shocked. After all, the things written in their letter were things they had prayed about.

In verse 4, Paul communicates to Philemon that when Paul prays he gives thanks to God for Philemon.

Before he asks Philemon for anything, or shares his concerns, or even begins to deal with the complicated situation of Onesimus, Paul first assures Philemon that he cares about him.

The group of the concerned members had never once communicated that they were thankful when they prayed for me. So if they were not grateful to God for me, what were they doing before God concerning me?

Can you guess?

They were blaming me, just as they had done with the previous pastor.

Who wants to be accused, put down, reprimanded, criticized, or even corrected? It is not that we don't need people to do these things with us, but we tend to take it or hear it only when we know that those doing it genuinely care about us. And the only way we know that people care about us is that they say and show it repeatedly.

So, perhaps you have concerns you want to

bring to your spouse, your parents, your kids, your boss, or your pastor. If you have not repeatedly communicated that you care about them in a multitude of ways, you would be better off keeping your concerns to yourself. Why? The people you want to help with your advice will not be able to hear what you say. They will react defensively or maybe even go on the attack. You must first work on communicating that you care about them.

How?

Start by actually praying for them. And I don't mean that you pray that God would change them into an image of your liking. Thank God for them as they are. Find something in them for which to give thanks.

Thanking God for someone does two things:

One, thanking God for someone helps you, the one doing the thanking, start to think of positive things about this person. Maybe you could be thankful for some aspect of their character. Or you could be grateful for the good things they have done for you or others. Find something to be thankful for.

Two, thanking God for someone will force you to humble yourself before God concerning this person. It is hard to thank God for someone and at the same time think negatively about them. When you pray to God for a person, you are in effect inviting the all-knowing, all-forgiving One, the One who knows both of you - the good, the bad and the ugly - to sit in on the relationship. And in His presence you are less likely to find fault with the other person.

After you have prayed for someone for awhile, find a way to communicate that you have been praying for them, not that God would change them, but that God would bless them.

His name was Tom. Our church in Vancouver rented office space above his sound studio. We often tried to get Tom to come to church, but he saw no need for it.

I liked Tom, and I liked music, so we often talked.

One day he confided in me that his sister was sick, and he was quite worried about her. I told him I would put her in my ACTS. He looked at me puzzled, but I just left it there.

A week later, I asked about his sister, and he told me the report from the labs came back negative - good news. I told him I was not surprised as I had put her in my ACTS.

He worked up the nerve and asked me what this ACTS thing was.

So I took out my Day Planner, which had ACTS sheets in it for every day. Each ACTS sheet had the headings: Adoration, Confession, Thanksgiving, and Supplication (one's needs). The idea was to write something every day under these headings as one's prayer to God.

So, I showed Tom every ACTS sheet of every day since I had told him I would pray for him and his sister. He could read his name and concern in my prayer journal, day after day. It was the black and white.

T impressed that he asked me t ACTS sheets.

at someone is positive- can't help but feel like d when a person feels pen to you.

S for people, especially ve issues. Never criticize someone you are not in

One more t nicated that he thanked God fo whenever his name came up in his praye. To communicate that you thank God for someone is to honor them. It is like a teacher or a coach thanking the parents for the outstanding performance of their son or daughter. In the process, both the parents and the child feel honored.

Maybe you could go pray every day for people in a section of your contact list on your phone.

Questions:

Philemon 1: 4 I always thank my God as I remember you in my prayers...

Philippians 1:3 I thank my God every time I remember you.

Colossians 1:3 We always thank God, the Father of our Lord Jesus Christ, when we pray for you ...

Step One: Relationship - Build it!

> *1 Thessalonians 1:2 We always thank God for all of you and continually mention you in our prayers.*
>
> *2 Thessalonians 1:3 We ought always to thank God for you, brothers and sisters, and rightly so, because your faith is growing more and more, and the love all of you have for one another is increasing.*
>
> *2 Timothy 1:3 I thank God, whom I serve, as my ancestors did, with a clear conscience, as night and day I constantly remember you in my prayers.*

1. Paul had a habit of communicating with the people to whom he wrote letters that he was thankful to God for them. Notice he did this at the beginning of each letter (for example, in the letter to Philemon, the Colossians, the Thessalonians, and Timothy). Later in each of these letters, he deals with some difficult relationship issues. In effect then, he builds the relationship before finding fault. Why do people often find fault first, and then try to salvage the relationship when this doesn't go well?

2. Even if you never told the person that you were praying for them, what would your prayer for them accomplish? Why do it?

3. What does telling the person that you are

praying for them accomplish? Why do it?

4. When someone communicates that they are thankful for you and are praying for you, how does it make you feel?

5. How would praying for a person and telling them you are thankful before God for them help when some complicated relationship issue comes up in the future between the two of you?

***STEP ONE:* Relationship - Build it.**

5. Communicate something positive about the other person.

Did you ever look closely at a penny?

It was my fifth-grade art class back in '66. We had to make something out of paper mache. Most of my classmates plastered balloons with the sticky mixture of paper, water, and flour to make baskets, masks and various animals (mostly pigs).

I happened to have a penny in my pocket and took it out and looked at it. I began to fashion a head. Next came the body covered with a long overcoat and pants. I finished my creation with shoes. Oddly, the shoes were the

---

Philemon 4-5
I always thank my God as I remember you in my prayers, because I hear about your love for all his holy people and your faith in the Lord Jesus.

hardest part. I had created a two foot high, paper mache Abraham Lincoln. It was incredible. At least, I thought so. Many of my classmates did too.

But what did my art teacher think?

She made one little comment, a comment that changed how I have thought about myself since she made her comment. She said, "Steve, **you are very creative**."

Notice that her comment was not so much about my work but more about me as a person.

From that day on I thought of myself as a creative person. Years later in college, when professors handed back the various papers that I had to write, I never cared much about the grade. What I looked for was the comment, "Very creative."

Was I born creative? Maybe. Did I know it before my teacher told me? No way.

What do you do well? How do you know that you do it well? How do the people close to you know what they do well? When is the last time you told your son or daughter, spouse or friend that you see something good in them?

Most of us are excellent at finding fault with those around us. And when we communicate what we have found, we do so "for their own good."

But is this really what people need? To be told where they fall short?

Isn't it often true that if you don't tell some-

> Who in your life made a little comment that made all the difference in your life?

one their fault, someone else will. There are people lined up to point out mistakes.

But who is going to say something positive? Once in awhile, people need to know what they are doing right.

If you say something positive on a repeated basis to someone, you will not only build that person up, but you will also develop a strong, positive relationship with that person.

So Paul, before getting into the tricky problem of what to do with Onesimus, makes sure that he communicates the positive things he has heard about Philemon. Paul builds up Philemon so that Philemon is feeling positive about himself, and in the process Paul creates a positive relationship with Philemon.

Paul says positive things to Philemon in two particular areas: Philemon's faith in God and his love for people.

God and people.

Twenty years ago a friend of mine, Henry Reyenga, and I were trying to come up with a new way to introduce Christianity to someone. We came up with this question: **What is your spiritual dream?**

How would you answer this question?

We asked it of everyone we met. We asked it everywhere we went. Since we were working for the Bible League International at the time, "everywhere we went" was all around the world.

Interestingly, no matter who we asked or where we asked it, everyone gave the same answer.

Some said their dream was to find the truth, others to be one with nature, many to have a great marriage or family, and one guy told me he wanted to be one with whales.

Now these sound like many different answers, but they all fall into two categories: God and people. The same two categories Paul commented on regarding Philemon. It would seem that **people's spiritual dream** (their ultimate dream) has to do with a connection to...

God and people.

Is this true of your spiritual dream as well?

You are still wondering about the guy who wanted to be one with the whales, aren't you?

Think about it. A person who wishes to be one with the whales more than likely believes in the whole "god is in everything and everything is a part of god" New Age way of seeing things. So the "I want to one with the whales" comment is just another way of saying, "I want to be one with God." What that means is that the whale lover and I have the same dream - to connect with God. We just disagree on who that God is.

So, in my opinion, all people are born with a dream, a desire to connect in a meaningful way to a god of some sort and the people around them.

But, though the dream is there, many are frustrated in realizing this dream. Why?

Go to Genesis 3. Though Adam and Eve

Step One: Relationship - Build it!

lack nothing living in a garden paradise, we see them disobeying God by doing what was forbidden. The result: They are ashamed of their nakedness and hide from each other. And when God comes around they, in fear and guilt, hide from Him.

They hide from God and people.

There it is again, our spiritual dream to connect with God and people. But sin makes us feel small, ashamed, lacking, imperfect, guilty and sends us into **hiding** from God and the people around us. What we want is the very thing from which we hide.

Where in your life are you hiding from people and/or God?

By the way, what we want, the dream of connecting in a meaningful way to God and people, is what God wants for us and even commands of us.

The Ten Commandments. Some see these as burdens, a bunch of do's and don'ts. But if you step back and take a broad view of them, you will discover they are nothing more than a prescription for the spiritual dream we all seek. What was that again? To connect in a meaningful way with God and people.

Take a look at the first four commandments. Each of them gives us insight into how to better relate to God. The next six commandments are how to have a healthy relationship with the people around us.

So, wonder of wonders, God only commands what we already want.

But sin - and the shame, guilt, and the brokenness that sin causes - keeps us hiding from the dream we seek.

Jesus' death and resurrection take us from hiding and reconcile us to God and people.

Paul, as he communicates something positive about Philemon, chooses these two areas:

1. Philemon's faith in **God**, and

2. The good he has done with **people**.

In other words, Paul is saying, "Philemon, I have heard from others that you are well on your way to your spiritual dream. How blessed you are."

If you want to build a positive relationship with someone, start the process by recognizing and communicating to this "someone" how God, because of the death and resurrection of Jesus and through the power of the Holy Spirit, is working to help this person fulfill their spiritual dream.

Communicating something positive is probably the most effective thing that I do as a Pastor. I actively look to **catch people doing something good**. In what areas do I look to accomplish this? In people's relationship with God and other people.

So if, for example, I see a young person who is faithful in their participation in church activities, I will find a moment to say something like, "I noticed you are very serious about God and His church. Keep it up because God ultimately is looking for people like you to carry out His

With whom do you need to work on catching them doing something good?

purpose." Notice this is the God connection.

Or when I see a parent doing all they can to keep their young children in line, I will say, "I see you have your hands full. Parenting is hard, but I've noticed that you do it with consistency and grace. It is not easy to be both strict and forgiving at the same time, but I see you doing it, and I just want to applaud your efforts. And I want you to know that even if you do not see progress day to day, believe me, your efforts will be rewarded." Notice this is the people connection.

Look for opportunities to say something positive to your spouse, your children, the people at work, at church, and in your neighborhood.

More Examples:

To your spouse: "I know I often take it for granted, but there are times when I am amazed at how well you... manage the household, care for me, make life exciting, take charge and lead, put God first in everything, organize our lives, etc."

To your kids: "I know I spend a lot of time telling you what to do and often give you the impression that you never do things quite right, but to tell you the truth, you are better at... school work, sports, concern for others, personal walk with God, etc... than I was at your age."

To your co-workers: "Have I ever said I like working with you? You are... fun to work with, a team player, good at solving problems, etc."

A few suggestions on how to do this:

When you want to make an impact by communicating something positive, do so by looking them in the eye. The eye is a window to the heart.

Sometimes words spoken become more personal when accompanied by a physical touch. Maybe a handshake or a pat on the back.

One last tip: When you say something positive, be specific. Don't just say, "You are a great person" or "I like working with you" or "You are gifted and talented." Tell them why you think they are a great person, why you like working with them, and why you believe they are gifted and talented.

Questions:

1. How does giving positive feedback help the person receiving it?

2. What does it do for the person giving it?

3. What does it do for the relationship between the two?

4. Paul is challenging Timothy in these verses: *1 Timothy 4:12 Don't let anyone look down on you because you are young, but set an example for the believers in speech, in conduct, in love, in faith,*

and in purity. Until I come, devote yourself to the public reading of Scripture, to preaching and teaching. Do not neglect your gift, which was given you through prophecy when the body of elders laid their hands on you.

What positive things is Paul saying about Timothy if you read between the lines?

5. How is giving people responsibility a way of communicating something positive to them?

6. With whom do you have a hard time communicating something positive? Why?

7. When was the last time someone said something positive about you? How did it make you feel?

STEP ONE: Relationship - Build it

6. Communicate how blessed this person is.

Paul is building the relationship he has with Philemon so that, in the end, both of them will be able to deal with the complicated, potentiality divisive issue of Onesimus.

So why **verse 6**? How does this verse build the relationship?

Let me ask you a few questions that might help you think about this. What happens when you deal with people who think they are blessed? Are they easier to deal with or harder? Are they more likely to be patient and listen to your side of some issue or less likely? Are

Philemon 6 (ERV) I pray that the faith you share will make you understand every blessing we have in Christ.

Step One: Relationship - Build it!

they more inclined to compromise to keep the peace or more liable to dig their heels in against you?

How about the other way. How easy is it to deal with people who, instead of feeling blessed, feel that life has treated them unfairly and that they deserve much better than they are getting?

Yeah, you know the answers to these questions.

So, how do you get someone to stop feeling sorry for themselves, to stop obsessing on what they lack or don't have, and to stop keeping track of who owes them? Conversely, how do you get someone to recognize what they have and ultimately how blessed they are?

How does Paul do it? Paul starts out in verse 6 with the words, "I pray..." He puts what he is going to say in the context of prayer. Why would he do this?

Prayer is not just talking and listening to God. It is a way in which we become super cognizant of His presence. God is, of course, always there, but we are not always aware of His presence. **Prayer** is a way that we remind ourselves and those around us that God is in on what we are doing.

Try praying with someone and see if that act of prayer

"I pray..." puts God in the room. With God in the room, Philemon is more likely to think about what he has, not what he doesn't have. With God in the room, Philemon is more likely to be less accusatory and more introspective of his own faults.

In a complicated relationship with another person, always invite God into the room.

What does Paul pray? That Philemon would share his faith.

Of course, since there is a church in Philemon's home, Philemon has already done this. So maybe Paul is trying to get Philemon to think about or remember some occasions where he has shared his faith.

So what would be the point of that? Think about a time you shared your faith with someone. Maybe you invited a non-church going friend to church and they came. Or maybe, after so many years of discipling your children, one of them came up to you and said that they wanted to confess their faith in Jesus publicly. Or maybe you went on a mission trip and you helped someone get a new house. How did sharing your faith make you feel?

My guess is you felt blessed. That is what one feels when one does something positive for someone else. Blessed. And I think one feels blessed for two reasons:

One, if you are blessing someone, it means that someone is most likely worse off than you. And if they are worse off than you, then when you are helping them, you begin to realize that you could have it much worse than you do. Their need is in stark contrast to your ability to help. What a blessing to be able to help!

Second, the act of helping someone gives

> *doesn't make you more humble, more gracious in terms of your attitude towards the other person.*

the helper a positive view of themselves. "I am a leader. I am somebody. I make a difference. I am an important contribution to the world. I help make good things happen in the Kingdom of God."

Can you see why Paul would want Philemon to think of himself in this way? Imagine if you actively tried to get the people close to you to think of themselves as important contributors to the Kingdom of God?

One final thought: There is an old saying in the secular world: "You don't know what you have till it is gone."

In the Christian world, we might say it this way: "You don't know how you have been blessed until you share the blessing with others."

Questions:

1. Why is it difficult to deal with a relationship issue when you are feeling abused, taken advantage of, or overlooked?

2. Why does helping someone make you feel good?

3. Is it possible to say, after reading Philemon 1:6, that a person doesn't understand his or her faith until that faith is shared with someone else?

4. When did you experience the truth of

question 3?

5. What are some common ways that a person can share their faith?

6. Who in your world needs a blessing? How can you be that blessing?

Philemon 7 (NIV) Your love has given me great joy and encouragement, because you, brother, have refreshed the hearts of the Lord's people.

STEP ONE: Relationship - Build it!

7. Communicate how much this person has done for you.

I went bowling for the first time in 20 years last weekend. Out of three games, my highest score was a 96. In college, I averaged 165. It was frustrating.

I had a good excuse for my poor play. I had rotator cuff surgery two months before and, therefore, had to use my left hand. I am not left-handed. Still, I thought I would do better.

As I played (poorly) I noticed that one thing has changed in the bowling world from 20 years ago - scoring is automatic. I wonder if young people growing up with electronic score-keeping know how the scoring in bowling works.

Though score-keeping in the bowling world has changed, some things are still the same. You still get to see and hear the ball knock the pins over. And it is still loud. It is cataclysmic. You get instant feedback. And by making adjustments based on the feedback, performance improves.

Imagine what bowling would be if you never saw or heard the ball hit the pins? Not only would the game be boring, but you would never improve. You would never know if what you were doing made a difference.

The people in your life - those you live with, those you work with, those you play with, and those you worship with - will only know the positive impact that they have and are making in your life if you tell them.

While going to seminary, I taught catechism (basic Christian doctrine) to a bunch of uninterested seventh graders. I felt like I was bowling in the dark with the sound turned off. I just couldn't connect. They were often rude and uncooperative. I felt like I was **throwing gutter balls** in every class session.

When has this happened to you?

Four years later, after finishing a chapel talk in the same Christian high school that I attended years ago, I was about to get in my car when out from the school came four young men calling my name. They were older, but I recognized them. They were from my seventh-grade catechism class. They thanked me

Step One: Relationship - Build it!

for our time together in the "old days" and told me that it made a big difference in their lives.

I would never have guessed.

We often have no idea the effect we have had on people until someone tells us.

Hearing that you made a difference in someone else's life is the sweetest music there is. Remember, it goes back to our spiritual dream, which is to connect with God and to make a difference in the lives of the people around us.

Make a habit of telling the people in your life what they have done for you.

Tell your spouse how they have blessed you by providing money, making you laugh, keeping things in order, challenging you to try new things, making life exciting, calming things down, creating an environment of stability, dressing nicely.

Tell your bosses how they have blessed you by providing a job, giving you new challenges, believing in you, making your life interesting, opening doors of opportunity, giving you permission to fail and try again, helping you explore possibilities.

Tell your children how they have blessed you by taking their responsibilities serious, working hard at school, giving joy to your life, making you proud of their accomplishments, living their lives as bold ambassadors for Christ.

As you read this you may be saying to yourself that your spouse, your boss, and your kids do not do these things. That the list I have

> *The other day at a Bible study everyone was asked what person in the past had the greatest spiritual influence on them. And when it was my wife's turn to speak, she said, "My husband." Priceless.*

given you just reminds you of all their faults and shortcomings.

Shame on you. Don't look for the negative. Is the negative there? Of course. But that is not what we are doing here. We are looking for good things. So stick with the program of looking for good things.

Search for good things to say about the lives of those around you with the same passion and enthusiasm that you would have if someone hid a bag of gold in your backyard and then told you that if you found it, you could have it. Because let me tell you, it is gold. It is better than gold.

Why do people tend to gravitate towards finding the negative in others instead of the positive?

My oldest son left with his wife and two kids (our grandkids) to live in Ecuador. The night before he left, my wife and I cried like babies (those that have had children move away know what this is about). I woke up at 3 am and I wrote a long letter to him, and I said all the things I wished I had said all along - positive, uplifting, father-to-a-son proud words.

Gold. Better than gold.

This is what Paul does with Philemon. He builds the relationship by communicating what Philemon has done for him.

Questions:

1. Sometimes it is hard to know if the people around us feel blessed by what we try to do for them. Why is it good, once in

awhile, to hear how well we are doing in blessing them?

2. *Philippians 4:10,15-16,18-20 I rejoiced greatly in the Lord that at last you renewed your concern for me. Indeed, you were concerned, but you had no opportunity to show it... 15 Moreover, as you Philippians know, in the early days of your acquaintance with the gospel, when I set out from Macedonia, not one church shared with me in the matter of giving and receiving, except you only; for even when I was in Thessalonica, you sent me aid more than once when I was in need... 18 I have received full payment and have more than enough. I am amply supplied, now that I have received from Epaphroditus the gifts you sent. They are a fragrant offering, an acceptable sacrifice, pleasing to God. And my God will meet all your needs according to the riches of his glory in Christ Jesus. To our God and Father be glory for ever and ever. Amen.*

How do you think Paul's words of thanks affected the church at Philippi?

3. Who in your life blessed you in a way that made a difference? How might you tell them that they made a difference in your life?

4. Why is it more effective to tell someone

some positive thing they did for you as opposed to just telling them something positive about them?

5. One excuse people give for not telling people what they have done for them is that no one has done this for them. "Why should I compliment this person when that person has never complimented me?" What role does fairness and unfairness play in the execution of communicating to others how much they have done for you?

STEP TWO: Influence - Use it!

1. Appeal to a higher motive.

> Philemon 8-9a Therefore, although in Christ I could be bold and order you to do what you ought to do, yet I prefer to appeal to you on the basis of love.

The quickest way to get someone to do what you want is to order them. Paul begins verse 8 by reminding Philemon that he, Paul, could get what he wants by simply ordering him.

However, to be successful with this "tell people what to do" type of motivation means you need the authority and the power to execute the consequences of obeying or disobeying.

Parents use this kind of motivation with their kids all the time. And it works, sort of.

A mom and dad were grocery shopping with their 3-year-old son. The son was supposed to sit and behave himself in the shopping cart.

But he kept standing up. Each time he did, one of the parents would tell him to sit down. Finally, the dad said to his little boy, "If you don't sit down we will take you out of here to the car." Their little boy sat down, but as he did so, he muttered, "I may be sitting down on the outside, but I am standing up on the inside."

No one likes it when someone **tells them what to do**. This form of motivation assumes that the one being told cannot evaluate and decide what is the best course of action and cannot be trusted to make the decision. In short, if you tell someone what to do, you are treating them like a child. Even children do not like being treated like children.

> This is the authoritarian form of motivation. How well or not does this form fit your personality?

A better way to motivate is by example.

If you want your kids to love church and consistently go, then you must love church and consistently go. If you are often missing from church, finding fault with the Pastor's sermon, and constantly complaining about what church leaders do, don't be surprised if your kids, when old enough to make a decision regarding the church, stop going.

If you want your children to have a vibrant daily walk with God, then they need to see you in prayer and in the Bible every day.

Some parents think that they can get away with this thinking: "Do as I say, not as I do." That does not work. What you say is credible only by what you do.

> This is the example

Being an example of what you want others to

form of motivation. How well or not does this form fit your personality?

be and do is a powerful motivating tool, but it is not a slam dunk.

We rented a gym for the church plant I was leading in Vancouver, Canada. We had to set up (and take down) a stage, chairs, banners, lights, and a sound system every week. We did this the whole nine years I was there. Every year it seemed we needed a new system of volunteers to make this happen.

One year, we the leadership board decided to be an example to the rest of the church, an example of humility and service. We would do the set up with our families for an entire year. So, we leaders had to not only do all the leading, but we had to do set up as well. It was a tough year, but we wanted to be a good example.

We did it. One year. Setting up and taking down. Did it make recruiting new volunteers any easier than before? Not one bit.

Sometimes being a good example is not enough. People, in general, are very quick to take all that others are doing for them for granted. So when you as a parent, a boss, or a church leader have humbled yourself, have gone out and done what you are now asking others to do, and then find out no one cares, most of us turn to the third motivational strategy - guilt.

Guilt, as a motivating strategy, is easy to employ when you are disappointed and perhaps even a bit angry at the lack of cooperation you are getting from those around you.

It looks like this:

Parent: "After everything I do for you, house, clothes, food, vacations, cable TV (and the list goes on and on), this is how you treat me? I ask one little thing of you, and you can't be bothered."

Boss: "I pay you a fair wage. I give you health benefits. You get paid time off. As a company, we are barely breaking even. And all I expect from you is that you do your best. Is that too much to ask for?"

Friend: "When you want to do something I always go along with it. But the one time I wish to do something different, you don't want to do it."

Pastor: "You don't give much money to the church. You don't have time to help out. You are not faithful in your devotions or consistent with your church attendance. And this, after Jesus died on the cross for you."

Guilt hurts. It hurts so much that we never let the guilt we feel sit very long in our hearts. We turn it into anger, anger-in or anger-out. Anger-in is depression. Anger-out is some form of blame or justification.

Here is the point. **Guilt**, and the anger-in or anger-out that it leads to, does not motivate the people around you to do as you want.

So how does Paul begin to motivate Philemon toward his way of thinking in terms of the runaway slave Onesimus? Paul has the power and position to order Philemon to do as he

This is the guilt form of motivation. How well or not does this form fit your personality?

wants, but he tells Philemon he doesn't wish to motivate him in this way. Instead, Paul appeals to a higher cause.

The best motivation, the kind that inspires people to do something that may require some sacrifice, comes when a person sees a worthwhile cause behind what is being asked. This is especially true when the goal is bigger than the people involved.

Soldiers are willing to die for their friends and country. Parents are willing to work long hours at a job they don't like for the sake of their family. College kids are prepared to eat ramen noodles for a few years to earn a degree that they believe will help them get a job that might help them make some positive difference in the world. Missionaries are willing to give up their culture and the comforts of home to reach people that don't know Christ.

Paul wants Philemon to do something, not just for Paul, and not just because Paul is the one asking, but for the sake of love - the love of God- something bigger than Paul or Philemon.

So you want to motivate someone to do something for you. Resist just telling them what to do. Don't just be an example you hope they will follow. And most of all, don't resort to making them feel guilty. Instead, try to communicate the greater cause behind the thing you are asking them to do.

Parents, instead of asking your kids to clean the garage, ask them to contribute to the cause of your great family.

Teachers, instead of just giving assignments, give them "this is possibly going to change your future" challenges.

Spouses, instead of complaining about the other not doing their share, invite them to join you in the God-ordained mission of becoming the unique partnership that God had in mind when He brought you two together.

Pastors, instead of complaining that no one gives his or her very best to church, invite people to join you in the greatest enterprise the world has ever known.

Here is the secret to doing this. Whenever you are about to ask somebody to do something or complain to someone that he or she is not doing something, stop a moment and ask yourself: What greater thing is this ask or complaint regarding? Why, ultimately, am I wanting this person to do something? *Pay attention here!!!!!*

Oh, and here is a hint to answering this last question: it is not all about you. The greater thing cannot be about you. It can be about us. It can be about God. It can be about some cause. But if the only reason you want someone to do something is because it is about you, good luck.

Questions:

1. Can you give an example of a time you tried to motivate someone by just ordering them to do something?

2. Can you give an example of a time you tried to motivate someone by example?

3. Can you give an example of a time you tried to motivate someone by guilting them?

4. Which technique is your "go to" in motivating people to do what you want? Order them? Give a good example? Guilt them? Appeal to a higher cause? Why?

5. If our desire to motivate is selfish, the people around us can sense it. But if our desire to motivate is something "beyond us," something "greater than us," then those we are trying influence will be more likely to respond in a positive way. Who are you attempting to influence these days and how could you appeal to a higher cause? (Let the group help you figure this out).

STEP TWO: Influence - Use it!
2. Communicate your needs in the language of the other's needs.

Onesimus, the runaway slave, appears on the doorstep of Philemon. He was caught and became a prisoner who deserved punishment. These were the thoughts and perhaps the perspective of Philemon.

Paul, in his letter, now uses the same "prisoner" language to talk about himself. Paul, like Onesimus, is a prisoner twice over of the Romans and God. Paul talks to Philemon in the same language as Philemon is thinking.

If a parishioner is complaining about the leadership not being open to using his gifts,

> Philemon 9b-10 It is as none other than Paul—an old man and now also a prisoner of Christ Jesus— that I appeal to you for my son Onesimus, who became my son while I was in chains.

> Romans 12:6 We have different gifts, according to the grace given to each of us ...
>
> 1 Corinthians 12:6 In his grace, God has given us different gifts for doing certain things well ...

you could respond with the language of gifts from **Romans 12** and **1 Corinthians 12**.

Or let's say that my wife is complaining to me that she feels like an unpaid maid in our household. But let's say that I also feel unappreciated for all the work that I do at the church. We both feel the same. How should I respond?

First, I need to listen to her, or nothing good is going to happen. After listening and actively trying to understand her, I can then offer to do whatever it is that would help her feel better about the whole situation. When it is finally my turn to express how I feel, I should use the same language that she used. I might say something like how I feel the family sees me as an unnecessary butler, not the owner of the house.

> A metaphor is a figure of speech in which a word or phrase is applied to an object or action that it does not literally denote in order to imply a resemblance; for example, he is a lion in battle.

Why is this important? It shows you have been listening. When people use **metaphors** to describe how they feel, they are into that metaphor world. Why not join them in that world rather than trying to get them to leave their metaphor world to enter a brand new one?

Everyone speaks their unique language, and if you hope to influence friends and tactfully get along with people, you have to learn the other's language. You have to come to the negotiation table knowing each person has their own perspectives, needs, and expectations.

Okay, easy enough. But here is what makes this difficult. Sometimes people say one thing, but they mean something else. They use one language, but they mean another.

A parishioner makes a comment about the color of the new carpet I am promoting at church, and I naively think we are talking about the carpet. But what she is talking about is that her sense of belonging and personal significance took a beating when no one sought out her opinion on this matter.

My wife complains that I left the cupboard door open, but she is really saying that she feels unappreciated and taken for granted.

A friend jokes that you are never on time, but what he is really saying is that he feels disrespected by you when you are late - as if his time is somehow less valuable than yours.

Philemon owned Onesimus and then lost him. He probably felt like someone stole Onesimus from him. Paul understands this, but he wants Philemon to know that if Philemon takes Onesimus back, Paul, the old man with the **needs** of an old man, will feel like someone stole Onesimus from him as well.

Each person in a conflict has their unique way of seeing the situation. And both parties must learn and appreciate the other's perspective if they hope to find a solution.

Onesimus was meeting the needs of Paul in Rome. Maybe you have a potential conflict situation. Try to see things from their perspective before saying yours.

Step Two: Influence - Use it!

Questions:

1. Why do you think Paul mentions that he is an old man?

2. Why do people use metaphors to describe how they feel about a situation?

3. In order to communicate your needs in the language of the other's needs, you must first listen and try to understand the other's needs. Why is this hard to do?

4. Can you give an example of how you recently did not first listen to the needs of the other before you communicated your needs?

5. Why don't we often have the patience to listen to the needs of the other person before communicating our needs?

6. On the positive side: Why is it that people are more willing to try and understand your needs only after you have demonstrated a desire to understand their needs?

7. What person in your life do you need to spend more time listening to?

STEP TWO: Influence - Use it!
3. Appeal to mutual benefits

"I get something; you get something."

"I scratch your back; you scratch mine."

"What is good for the goose is good for the gander."

"Do unto others as you would have others do to you."

"Give and take."

"50/50."

"Win/win."

There are a lot of ways to say it. And it sounds like a fair deal. But how is this love?

Philemon 11
Formerly he was useless to you, but now he has become useful both to you and to me.

Love is not always 50/50.

At the beginning of Paul's letter to Philemon, he calls Philemon "beloved" or in some translations "friend." The actual Greek word that Paul uses is "agape" which is often translated as "love."

Agape love is unconditional love. When my wife and I got married, we pledged unconditional love to each other. "I will love you no matter what I get in return." Agape seems like the best kind of love.

But there is another kind of love that is found in the Bible. The Greek word is "**eros**."

> *Sounds kind of selfish doesn't it?*

This love is a love that says, "I love something because it does something for me."

"I love pizza because pizza satisfies my hunger and makes me happy." Eros, unlike agape, is love with conditions.

Most friendships are built on eros. "You are my friend because I enjoy being with you. I get pleasure from you. And more than likely, you call me friend because you get something from me."

Eros friendship is a give and take relationship. It is a mutual benefit kind of thing. For example, you go out to dinner with your friend and he offers to buy lunch. Great. Next time you will pick up the check. This picking-up-the-check thing goes back and forth without either of you keeping track, and at the end of the year, you both instinctively know that it is close to a wash. If, on the other hand one person starts paying more than the other without there being a reason for it, the relationship slips from friend and friend to sponsor and dependent.

Friendships, at least in the beginning, are built on **shared interest**. I like to golf, and you like golf. We like to golf together. Or we like classic cars, or art, or travel, or work, or philosophy, or photography, or kids, or whatever else. You get the picture.

> Shared interest is different than being selfish. How is this so?

Eros friendships are somewhat selfish. But they have to be mutually selfish. Both partners are not only getting what they want from the other, but each is trying to give to the other what the other wants. This takes a lot of work.

For example, if your friend has a business where he sells things and you want $10 off the regular price on something he sells, you are, in effect, asking your friend to give you $10. If he were to treat you the same, he would be the one coming to you and asking if you don't mind, because you are his friend, paying $10 **more** than the regular price. You would then in effect be giving him $10.

> Do you get this?

The point is it goes both ways. It is a mutual thing. Sometimes I am the one sacrificing and sometimes you are the one sacrificing. And it averages out.

But someone might ask, "What about agape love, the unconditional love then? How does this love fit in?"

I met my wife in college. I was attracted to her. And she, believe it or not, slowly, over

Where in your life has eros love become agape love?

Why is it hard to not to be selfish or self-absorbed when it comes to what we want from other people?

time, became attracted to me. We loved being together. We enjoyed sharing some of the same interests. We got married, in large part, because we each had much to gain from this new partnership. We both benefited. But what began as **eros love became agape love** when we made our wedding vows. Mutual or conditional love became unconditional love.

The point is eros love has a place in relationships, and Paul now appeals to it in his relationship with Philemon.

Onesimus means "useful." Paul in effect is saying to Philemon that Onesimus, the useful one, became useless to Philemon when he ran away. But now that Onesimus is a Christian, he has become useful again - to Paul, and perhaps, even more useful to Philemon.

You want your spouse, your kids, a friend, or someone at work to do something for you. Instead of badgering, guilting, and manipulating them into doing what you want, spend some time figuring out what those around you want.

What does your wife want from you? What would your boss get excited about if you were to do it?

How can you be a positive force in the wants and needs of those around you? And how might these things help you get what you want?

Sometimes our wants can line up. "We both get what we want."

Sometimes it just takes a little tweaking. "If

we change this or that, we both can get what we want."

Sometimes we will have to compromise. "Let's meet in the middle." Neither of us gets exactly what we want, but it's close enough.

Sometimes it will be an exchange. "You do this for me, and I will do that for you."

Some of you are saying to yourselves that you have tried this with the people close to you and it just doesn't work.

Why doesn't this always work?

Because we often sabotage the process. How? By not going for the **mutual benefit**. We pretend that we are interested in a mutual benefit, but we are just doing whatever it takes to get what we want.

Appealing to a mutual benefit is not just some technique that one can employ to get the other person to give you what you want. You must truly care about the other person's benefit.

> Why is it hard to not to be selfish or self-absorbed when it comes to what we want from other people?

Questions:

1. What does the name "Onesimus" mean?

2. The primary concern of Philemon was the loss of a slave who was useful but, after he escaped, became useless. Under Paul's influence, however, he became useful again both to Philemon and to Paul. Why is it easier to get "buy-in"

from someone you are trying to influence when you show them what they might gain in the bargain?

3. How are friendships built on mutual benefits?

4. What happens to a friendship when one person does most of the benefiting and the other does most of the giving?

Exodus 20:12 "Honor your father and your mother, so that you may live long in the land the Lord your God is giving you.

5. According to Exodus 20, what are parents supposed to get? What do sons and daughters get?

6. How do most of God's laws for us do something for God and something for us?

7. Can you think of a situation where you wanted something from someone but your approach to getting it was all wrong?

8. How might you rethink this situation in terms of mutual benefits?

STEP TWO: Influence - Use it!

4. Share your heartfelt feelings in the matter

My coworker's son stopped going to church soon after he got married. And even when kids came along (that would be my coworker's grandkids), things did not improve. In fact, the kids (grandkids) weren't even baptized.

My coworker did not know what to do. She, of course, prayed about the situation. She and her husband sometimes asked their son and family to go to church with them.

It was hard, they confessed, to talk directly to him about it. So they resorted to little pokes: "So, you are too good to go to church these

> Philemon 12
> I am sending him—who is my very heart—back to you.

Do you have people in your life that are close to you that have walked away from God and/or the church?

days?" Or little guilt trips: "It sure would be nice to be able to watch our grandkids in the Christmas program." Sometimes they would talk about the sermon at their church and how good it was in the presence of their son.

My heart ached for them. I often prayed with my coworker. One day I asked her if she and her husband had ever just poured out their hearts to their son.

She didn't know what I meant. "Of course we did," she replied.

So I asked a few questions to clarify: "In your heart of hearts, what are your fears about your son, your daughter-in-law and your grandkids?"

She thought for a bit and said, "That they have or will slowly reject Christ, and they will be separated from us for all eternity. That our grandkids will never know Christ."

"If you could share your heart with your son, what else would you say to him?" I continued.

She looked down. It got real quiet. Tears started to form in the corners of her eyes. She looked up and softly said, "You are my precious son. You are my life, my joy, my purpose. And my heart is breaking for you. I wake up in the middle of the night lost and afraid for you. I try to find you, but you are gone. I feel like I am losing you forever."

It was very touching. I felt her pain and sorrow. But I knew there was more. "What about your grandkids?"

"When they were born it was the greatest day of my life. They are my treasures. But they are missing out on everything we taught our kids. We do not share our most important connection - faith in Christ."

"What else could you tell your son and daughter-in-law?" I persisted.

"That we are sorry for any bad example we may have set. Our faith was not always genuine. We often just went through the motions. But now, we read the Bible together every day. We pray together. God shows up. He is real. He gives us what we need. We have a real sense of purpose together. And we want you to have the same thing."

"Okay," I responded, "Why don't you give your son a call. Ask him if you can meet at a park or a restaurant - just him and you. Tell him you want to share something vital. Don't tell him what is. Let him worry about it. Then meet with him and share, not your anger, frustration, and desires, but share with him your heart, your fears, your sadness, your hopes, and your dreams. Share your hurt with no agenda.

Your goal here is not to get him to do anything but to hear your heart, to feel the burden that you feel for his very soul. Then ask forgiveness for not modeling your personal walk with God very well during his growing up days, and then share how things have changed in your life - that you now have a real talking and listening relationship with a God that has be-

Who do you need to call?

come real to you."

It took a lot of courage, but **she made the call**, had the meeting, and was able to share her heart with her son. Guess what? He listened. He heard for the first time her heart. And he responded by coming back to faith and the church.

Some of you are thinking that sharing your heart is just not you. You don't care for all that touchy, feely stuff. You are a logical, straight-shooting, tell-it-like-it-is kind of person. And that is the way it is.

Paul was like that too. He was trained as a church lawyer, a Pharisee. In fact, before becoming a Christian, Paul was one of the top Pharisees in the Jewish world of his day. Pharisees made their living debating the finer points of Jewish religious law. He was a cold logic debater. But Paul, in his letter to Philemon, shares his heart.

Maybe there are people in your life, people close to you, that have hurt you, and you want to tell them about it. Or maybe there is someone you know well and care about that is struggling with some addiction - alcohol, drugs, gambling, anger, inappropriate Internet browsing, or gossip.

Again don't just read this book. You have to act on these principles if you want them to work in your life.

Share your heart. Don't blame. Don't get angry. Don't resort to sarcasm. Don't whine and complain. Share your heart. Share the love you have for this person that is causing your heart to break. Share your heart-brokenness in the matter.

Share your heartfelt feelings in the matter

Questions:

> *Philemon 1:12 I am sending him--who is my very heart--back to you.*

1. The word translated "heart" is literally "bowels" or "one's insides." Paul is telling Philemon that he is hurting to the very core of his being over sending Onesimus back to Philemon. Why do you think this situation caused Paul such pain?

2. We want to influence someone - a son, a daughter, a spouse, a friend, a co-worker, a church member - and we often do it poorly, often in anger, maybe with a demanding attitude or perhaps some guilt topped off with an argumentative spirit. A better way might be to share your heart. Tell the person what the situation is doing to you on the inside - the fear, the love, and the pain. Why do we often share concerns with another person poorly?

3. What is hard about sharing your heart with someone?

4. To whom and in what situation do you need to share your heart, your feelings?

Philemon 13-14
I considered keeping him with me so that he might serve me in your place during my time in prison because of the gospel.

However, I didn't want to do anything without your consent so

STEP TWO: Influence - Use it!

5. Suggest what you prefer but leave the decision up to them.

Letting people decide for themselves is one of the greatest people smart skills that you can learn. It is also the hardest to do.

You tell your teenage son that you would like him home before 11 pm. That is your preference. But you want to teach him responsibility, so you give him two options with consequences. Home before 11 pm means he is free to do as he wants on Saturday morning. Home after 11 pm means four hours of work.

He comes back at 11:30 pm. You meet him in the driveway. You get angry at him and read him the riot act for 15 minutes. You finish off sarcastically, "I hope you enjoy working because that is what you will be doing all day Saturday."

You walk away frustrated, angry, and feeling like a lousy parent. Your son walks away frustrated, angry, and feeling like you are a lousy parent.

What went wrong?

You gave him a choice. You would have preferred that he chose wisely and came home before 11 pm. But you gave him a choice, and your son made his choice. Honor it. Instead of unloading your frustration with his wrong choice for 15 minutes in the driveway, just acknowledge his choice.

"Son, I see you choose to work in the yard for four hours on Saturday. Great, I could use the help." Then walk away. Walk away with confidence that you made the right choice in letting your son experience the consequences of his decisions.

And your son? He will most likely walk away wondering if he made the right choice.

The issue here is control. To give someone a real opportunity to make a decision is to give up control.

But that is the real world. We don't control people. Even if you were to tell someone what to do, the person you are telling could choose to ignore you. Or worse choose to disobey.

And since you cannot control them, do like

that your act of kindness would occur willingly and not under pressure.

Step Two: Influence - Use it!

> *After reading these examples see if you can come up with examples of your own.*

Paul, let your desires be known and then, if possible, leave the decision up to them.

Examples ...

Spouse: "Honey, I would like to go to Europe on vacation, but I am going to let you decide."

Coworker: "From my experience it works better this way. But it is really up to you."

Friends: "I wouldn't mind going out for Chinese food, but why don't you decide."

Pastor: "If it were my marriage, I would at least go to counseling before breaking up. But it is up to you."

Parent: "If I were you, I would get up on time so you can catch the bus rather than have to walk all the way to school. But it is up to you."

What would happen if you started giving up control over the people in your life? Would people take advantage and trample over your wants and desires? Sometimes. But more often than not, when you let the other guy make the decision, he will respond in gratitude for the confidence and trust that you have placed in him. And in gratitude, he will then be inclined to do what you prefer or, at least, give your suggestion serious consideration. In short, they will seek ways to please you. They will treat you as you have treated them.

Try it out this week. In your home or at work. Find a situation where you want to offer advice or tell someone what to do. Instead, communicate what you prefer, but tell them that you trust them to make the right decision. It may be a bit scary to do this. You are giving up some of your control, but in the long run, you are helping those you are trying to lead take more ownership of their decisions.

Questions:

1. *Philemon 1:13-14 I considered keeping him with me so that he might serve me in your place during my time in prison because of the gospel. However, I didn't want to do anything without your consent so that your act of kindness would occur willingly and not under pressure.* If you are in a position of power (at work, at home, in a group), you can demand that people do things your way. Where in your life has this strategy not worked that well?

2. Paul makes it clear what he wants, but he totally leaves the decision up to Philemon. How often do you do this with your kids? The people at work? Your spouse? Your friends?

3. *Matthew 26:36 Then Jesus went with his disciples to a place called Gethsemane... Then he went a short distance farther and fell on his face and prayed, "My Father, if it's possible, take this cup of suffering away from me. However--not what I want*

but what you want."

With whom do you need to communicate openly and honestly how you feel about some issue, ultimately leaving its resolution in their hands?

STEP TWO: Influence - Use it!
6. Communicate the potential good in the problem.

They were new to the church. A husband, a wife, and two kids. I showed them how to read the Bible and pray and gave them the Bible reading plan that our whole church was following. They were willing to give it a try.

I invited them to the small group I was leading, a small group whose purpose was to support group members' walk with God in their personal lives, marriage, and family.

They came. It seemed to go well. There was a lot of great sharing and supporting.

The next meeting only the wife came. The

Philemon 15-16 Maybe this is the reason that Onesimus was separated from you for a while so that you might have him back forever— no longer as a slave but more than a slave— that is, as a dearly loved brother. He *is especially a dearly loved brother to me.*

husband was busy with a meeting.

The next small group meeting it was the wife only again. Another excuse for the husband.

The next meeting, again, the wife was alone. This time, when we asked where her husband was, she blurted out through tears, "My husband is back on cocaine."

Okay, now that is a problem. But there was good in the problem. We now knew what we were up against. Often in the church world, people's problems are kept hidden for years and years. Time is wasted. Emotional energy is spent. But no one knows what is the real issue.

It only took two small group meetings to find the problem.

In second grade, I had a hard time with reading and comprehending. I would read a short story and wouldn't be able to answer the simplest of questions about it. I was put in a "special" reading class with a few of my other reading-challenged classmates. I was not sure what progress we were making.

When as a parent you see your child struggling with school work, or with friends, or with health issues, it breaks your heart. You want to fix it.

After a few months in this special reading class, my teacher met with my parents to discuss my situation, my problem. The teacher told my parents that I just wasn't catching on and that maybe I never would. Then she said, or at least this is what my dad told me, "Teach him a trade; he'll never go to college."

Maybe **your problem** is not cocaine or reading issues. Maybe you struggle with ADHD. Or depression. Or a strong-willed child. Or debt. Or fear. Or boredom. Or health problems.

What might your problem be?

Well, my dad took my teacher's words as a challenge. He found some workbooks from a company, and both my younger brother and I had to do these workbooks every day. He gave us a dollar for every book we finished.

I don't know if these workbooks helped, but I do know that my dad's attitude, how he took a problem and made it a challenge, helped me go positively forward in my student career. By the way, my student career took me through four years of college and then another four years of graduate school.

The example of my father taking on a problem, my problem, and changing it into a challenge, became one of my greatest inspirations.

Problem or challenge. Which do you tend to focus on?

I mentioned the **example of Tom** and the ACTS sheets back in the Topic 1 - remember, he was the guy with the sound studio below our church office. Tom started coming to our church. He also started a music video production company. So we started making short church videos.

See page 57

One of our first videos went this way:

On the screen was a glass sitting all by itself on a chair filled with water to the halfway point. As the camera slowly zoomed in, a voice asked, "Is the glass half full or half empty?"

The camera kept zooming in on the glass, which eventually filled the whole screen. The voice answered the question, "Neither."

Then a hand introduced a new glass into the scene, about half the size of the first one. Another hand picked up the first glass and poured the water of this first glass into the smaller glass, filling it to the top. The voice-over continued, "The glass is neither half full nor half empty. It is just too big."

The video ended with these words scrolling across the bottom: "Brought to you by the church of lower expectations."

Now, I am all for expecting the best of people. In fact, that is one of the principles that we will look at in this book.

But sometimes we expect too much in the short term and too little in the long run.

We hope the car, the fridge, the electricity and the Internet work today. We expect our job to be there when we get to work tomorrow. We expect food on our table. We expect a degree of obedience from our kids and a bit of friendly conversation with our spouse. So when the car does not work or the Internet is down, or our son says something disrespectful, we can easily feel overwhelmed.

It is the unexpected problems that bring us down. But each unexpected problem has unrealized solutions as well. And therein is the good.

Questions:

1. *Philemon 1:15-16 Maybe this is the reason that Onesimus was separated from you for a while so that you might have him back forever-- no longer as a slave but more than a slave--that is, as a dearly loved brother. He is especially a dearly loved brother to me. How much more can he become a brother to you, personally and spiritually in the Lord!*

   Paul and Philemon have a problem. Runaway slaves merited death. But Onesimus, the slave, is now a Christian. Philemon is a Christian. Paul is trying to help Philemon see the good that can come out of this situation. How do you think Philemon heard all of this?

2. When facing a sensitive issue, why is there a tendency to focus on the negatives?

3. Why is it sometimes hard to focus on the positives?

4. Why is it even more difficult to concentrate on potential positives?

5. Where do you need to focus on the positives and potential positives?

Philemon
17 So if you consider me a partner, welcome him as you would welcome me.

STEP THREE: Commitment - Do it!

1. Make your request or suggestion with humility.

Paul has already suggested what he wants - that is to keep Onesimus as a helper. However, Paul is not pushing for his desire. But he now spells out in clear terms what he is willing to push for - that Philemon accept his runaway slave Onesimus as if he were Paul himself.

This was the point of Paul's letter. And it doesn't come until seventeen verses into it.

What does this tell you?

It should tell you that if you want to influence the people in your life, you need to work on the relationship you have with these people first.

And even when you have a good relationship with someone, you need to proceed with tact.

What is tact?

Tact is giving the other person space to disagree with you. Tact is giving the other person space so that they can tell you their point of view, freely and easily.

Try this: In the next conversation you have with someone you know well, make a note on how many times you or the other person states an opinion as if it were an established fact. It might be a conversation about how something works, or about the government, or other people, or what some church committee should or shouldn't do.

If you tried it, how did it go?

Notice how things are said. "The people at my work just don't have a clue."

"The government can't do anything right."

"John has no idea what he is doing."

"The building and grounds committee at church sure blew it with the color of the new carpet."

Now, perhaps when you say things like this you feel you are just telling the plain and simple facts. But why not say what you know - your facts - with some tact.

How do you say things with tact, and what does that do?

Tact is what Paul does. He finally gets to the point of his letter to Philemon, and how does he proceed? He uses the word "if." Paul says, "If you consider me a partner ..." The word "if"

Step Three Commitment: Do it!

gives space to Philemon. Space for Philemon to work out what he truly thinks about Paul's request.

Someone comes up to you and gives their opinion about what and how you should do something. And they tell you in a "this is the way it is" kind of manner. You either have to just go along with their suggestion or, if you don't want to do that, you must now engage that person in a battle.

When someone brings a strong opinion to the table, you either have to go with it, or you will need an equally strong comeback. If you do the former, you are like the little boy who was sitting down on the outside but standing up on the inside. If you do the latter, you will have a fight on your hands.

If only people would give their opinion with an "if."

How do you do that? Start an interaction like this ...

In my opinion ...

It seems to me ...

As I recall, it went this way ...

If you want my opinion ...

You make a good point, but here is another way to look at it.

Try these discussion starters out on people

Each one of these **discussion starters** give space to the other person. The person you are talking to can freely voice their concerns and objections without getting all emotional about it. Why? **You have given them space**.

We forget that most people are quite fragile and are easily threatened. Add to this that most do not like change and will, as a matter of course, be negative at any suggestion of change.

Time is needed.

So voice your concerns, your desires, your opinions in a way that preserves the ego of the other and gives them space to discuss and gradually come to your way of thinking.

Questions:

1. Philemon 1:17 *So if you consider me a partner, welcome him as you would welcome me.*

   Paul has told Philemon what he really would like - to keep Onesimus as a helper. Paul is not pushing for this desire. Instead, he spells out, in no uncertain terms, what he is willing to push for - that Philemon accept his runaway slave Onesimus as if he were Paul himself. How do you think Philemon reacted to this request?

2. Why do we often hint at or joke about or dance around what we really want to ask of someone, especially with those close

and see how it makes a difference. You will find that when you give people space, time to think, and even time to object to your proposal, more often than not they will eventually come to your way of thinking.

to us?

3. Instead of telling people exactly what we are thinking or wanting, we hope they will somehow just figure it out. Do you often do this?

4. Notice Paul makes his request only after he has spent a considerable amount of time building up his relationship with Philemon. Why is this a good idea?

5. Salespeople build a relationship just to make a sale (at least that is often our perception of salespeople). How do we do the work of building a relationship without doing so just to "make a sale"?

STEP THREE: Commitment - Do it!
2. Offer to help where you can.

Put your money and your effort where your mouth is.

Paul not only wants Philemon to forgive his runaway slave Onesimus for betraying Philemon, but Paul also wants Philemon to set Onesimus free. That will cost Philemon. And Philemon has already paid many times for Onesimus.

First, there was the cost of buying Onesimus. Then there was the cost of training him. After that, there was the cost of hunting for Onesimus when he escaped. Perhaps, added to this, was the cost of a replacement slave.

> Philemon 1:19a
> I, Paul, am writing this with my own hand. I will pay it back ....

Step Three: Commitment - Do it!

Onesimus would need money to carry out his escape plan, money he no doubt stole from Philemon.

And now Paul wants Onesimus set free?

But incredibly Paul offers to pay Philemon for his losses.

There is a saying that goes like this: Talk is cheap. If you believe in something, do something about it.

So often in a church there is a need for something - an addition, an upgrade to the sanctuary space, or new carpeting. Everyone will benefit from whatever is done, but not everyone actually pitches in with money or effort.

We just updated our sanctuary at the church I serve, and some people gave considerably towards the project in time or money or even both. **But many did very little in time or money.**

We completed the project, and now people see the vision and are excited about it. But it never would have happened if the few didn't go way beyond their share in the project.

Do I resent the people that didn't pitch in? No. We did not engage in the project first of all for the people. We did it because we thought the cause of Christ would be better served. We did it because we felt God was calling us to do it.

Sometimes the obstacle to people stepping out in faith and doing something is their extreme need for fairness.

"Last year, I worked an entire Saturday

When have you put a lot of effort into some communal project where you did most of the work? How did you end up feeling about it?

cleaning up the church yard. Someone else should do it this year."

"I already give more money to church than most people; someone else should take on this project."

"I already give 60% of the effort into this partnership; I'm not doing a percentage more."

The problem or dilemma is most people's self-perception is that they do more than others, and it is just **not fair** to expect even more out of them.

The only answer to this dilemma is not to care that it is unfair. Just do it whether it is fair or not. Do it because it is the right thing to do.

Where do you get the motivation to do this? Look at how God treats you. You don't deserve his grace; you are often guilty of seeking first your own kingdom and only giving God what you won't miss or what you can easily afford. But God still saves you anyway. Is that fair?

If you want something done, put yourself on the line. Commit yourself and invite others to help. If people are slow in helping, double your own efforts.

Don't sit around waiting for everyone to get on board. If you do, you may be sitting your whole life.

My first church was a country church. My salary was $15,500 a year, plus housing and utilities. At the time, I didn't know what we were going to do with so much money.

With whom do you have a 50/50 understanding that you feel is more like 60/40?

After the first year, the church leaders came around to ask how my wife and I were doing financially. We told them we were fine. So they did not recommend a raise that year.

Someone in our church did not think that was right, so they sent us an anonymous check for $2,000.

God taught me early on in my ministry that He will take care of my financial needs. Ever since then, I have never asked for or discussed my finances with any church that I served. I take whatever they decide to pay.

But back to my first church. It was growing, and I felt the church needed its first secretary to take care of some of the increasing demands. The church, in its 70-year history, had never had a secretary, and it seemed like a hard sell.

The cost was $4,000 a year. Back in 1984, that was, at least, $12,000 in today's money. I felt so strongly about getting a secretary that I offered my next year's raise and then some to pay for half of it. So I would pay half, and the whole rest of the church would pay the other half.

The proposal passed. After the meeting one of the church members came up to me and said, "I am surprised that it passed."

"Really," I responded incredulously. "Why wouldn't it pass?"

He said, "This church has got along fine for 70 years without a secretary, why would we need one now?"

Obviously, he didn't buy into or seriously consider the list of reasons for a church secretary that came with the proposal, so I took another tact. "Look at it this way. If I, your pastor, the one working at the church day by day, think that it is needed, and if I think it so strongly that I am willing to pay half the cost, then maybe the need is real. I mean, why would I pay for something that isn't needed?"

I looked him right in the eye. "I am willing to pay the cost of something that is for the benefit of the entire church, leaving the other half for the whole congregation. Why would you not just do it for my sake alone?"

He looked at me. Nothing to say. So I finished the conversation. "We have 500 people. If we divide the congregational cost for our new secretary by 500, it comes to $4 a person. So I am willing to pay $2,000, and all I am asking you to pay is $4."

Slam dunk.

I not only expected him to start waving the white flag of surrender but also to thank me profusely for my willingness to bear so much of the burden. Instead, he timidly said, "Well, I just didn't think we needed a secretary." And then he walked away.

As I look back, I should have been a bit more gracious. After all, the proposal passed. Most of the members apparently supported the proposal.

Step Three: Commitment - Do it!

Most people will respond positively to you when you, not only ask them for something, but also offer to help in the very thing you are asking. But not everyone will respond positively. Some just end up feeling guilty because of your generosity and then may turn that guilt into anger - toward you and toward whatever you are trying to accomplish.

We don't know how Philemon reacted to Paul's proposal. It really could have gone either way.

Maybe Paul's offer to pay any debt incurred by Philemon on account of what Paul was asking convicted Philemon to take Paul's desire seriously.

Or maybe Paul's offer to pay money to Philemon, money Paul did not in any way owe Philemon, may have left Philemon feeling guilty about the whole thing.

Or maybe Philemon felt like Paul was pushing him into a corner. If he accepted Paul's money, he would feel like a chump. If he refused Paul's money and kept Onesimus as a slave, he would be going against what Paul clearly wanted. So, Philemon had no choice but to set Onesimus free.

I think in the end it was the right thing for Paul to do. If you want something to happen, be the biggest supporter of the thing you want. In the end, something is going to get done.

Questions:

1. If Philemon sets Onesimus free, it will cost Philemon the price of a slave and more. Paul puts himself out on a limb offering to pay any and all costs. Why do you think Paul proposed to do this?

2. Paul puts his money where his mouth is. Why is this important if you want people to commit to your way of thinking and planning?

3. John 3:16 *For God so loved the world that he gave his one and only Son, that whoever believes in him shall not perish but have eternal life.*

   Paul is willing to sacrifice himself for the life and freedom of Onesimus. When someone is trying to lead, what role does the leader's willingness to sacrifice play in getting people to follow?

4. How are you applying this principle to your leadership?

STEP THREE: Commitment - Do it!

3. Gently remind them of what they owe you.

Never start a negotiation by talking about how much the other person owes you. Paul tells Philemon what Philemon owes him way at the end of his letter, after a lot of relationship building.

No one likes to be indebted to someone else. No one likes the word "debt."

And yet most of us have all kinds of debt. House, car, Internet, phone, and cable, just to mention a few. Anything that requires an ongoing monthly payment is debt.

Why do we have debt? Because we want to

> Philemon 1:19 I, Paul, am writing this with my own hand. I will pay it back—not to mention that you owe me your very self.

enjoy something before we have all the money for it. We are like children who cannot wait until Christmas to open our presents.

So we bring on much of the debt we struggle with, and what does this debt do to us? It enslaves us. The bank owns us. The cable and Internet companies own us. We now have to spend most of our time working, perhaps doing a job that does not inspire us, to pay our debts. This debt is negative debt.

But there is **positive debt**.

Jesus died on the cross to set you free from sin and death. You owe him your life. You are indebted to Him. If you are married, you promised to love, cherish and respect your spouse no matter what. You owe these things to your spouse. You are indebted. Children owe their parents. Friends do things for you, and you owe them. You are indebted to all these people.

The alternative is that you don't owe anybody anything, and nobody owes you. You are an island. Debt between friends is a good thing. It keeps us connected.

So Paul brings up the debt connection to Philemon. You can tell it is a risky thing to bring up because he says, "... not to mention that you owe me your very self." He says "not to mention," but then he goes on to mention it.

What is Paul talking about when he mentions Philemon's debt to him? Most scholars believe that either Paul brought Philemon to faith in Christ, or that Paul brought Epaphras

How have you seen good debt connecting you to the people in your life?

to the faith who then brought Philemon to faith in Christ. Either way, Paul is responsible, from the human point of view, for the salvation of Philemon.

Paul is establishing his authority here and is in effect saying to Philemon that he should consider Paul's request because Paul is the elder to Philemon.

Did you grow up with this tradition?

Respecting one's elders is or perhaps was a worldwide phenomenon. I am writing this chapter from Quito, Ecuador. My wife and I are visiting our son who married a girl from Ecuador. We have participated in several extended family celebrations, and at each one, the adults eat first. In the culture I live in, the kids eat first.

Paul, in a sense, uses the elder card with Philemon, but he does so in a culture that understands it. And even as he does this, he only does so after a whole lot of relationship building.

So what should you do? Someone owes you.

You have two options. One is to just be wronged. People, in general, will always think that they are owed more than they owe. We hate being indebted to someone so much that we will either do something about it to get rid of it or justify it (rethink all the events so that we do not owe but are owed). So, sometimes the thing to do is to accept the injustice and do what is best in the big picture.

The other option is to say something. This is

not easy. How do you tell someone who thinks you owe them that they, in fact, owe you? One approach is to humbly bring up the subject in a "let's make sure no one is being taken advantage of" manner.

You share your point of view, which you readily admit could be way off. Then they share their view in the same humble spirit. Hopefully, you can meet in the middle somewhere. The key to this approach is **humility**, and the willingness to admit you did not see things accurately.

Do you think you can do this?

Another approach is to tell them how you feel. For example, I might say to a co-worker, who is not pulling his/her weight regarding the work that must be done, something like this: "I want to share some frustrations that I am having in my relationship with you." (Notice I am not assigning blame). "I feel like I do quite a bit of the work around here, and then when I ask you for help, you never have the time, or you act like I am placing some incredible burden on you. Then I get angry, and I just do the work without you. I think you are a talented, gifted person, and so I just don't understand why this has become a problem for me."

Let's look at what I am doing. First, I am expressing my frustration and unhappiness. Then I am explaining why I feel this way. And finally, I end with saying something positive about the person and my confusion as to why this has become a problem.

One more thing. Notice that I am saying

Step Three: Commitment - Do it!

If you start blaming them, they are more than likely to respond in anger and won't hear a thing you say.

exactly what I think, but I am not assigning **blame**.

I have used this approach in many difficult situations, and it rarely fails to lead to a positive outcome.

So, when it comes to reminding people of what they owe you, do so only after a lot of relationship building, do so as humbly as you can, and do so as directly as you can. Or, decide not to do anything at all.

Questions:

1. *Philemon 1:18-19 I, Paul, am writing this with my hand. I will pay it back--not to mention that you owe me your very self. I do wish, brother, that I may have some benefit from you in the Lord; refresh my heart in Christ.*

   Notice this step is at the end. What would happen in a negotiation that you are having with someone you know if you started the conversation with what you think they owe you?

2. Paul is asking for what is owed him, but notice that Paul, in the verse preceding, offers to pay what Philemon may think is owed him. What does this fact tell you regarding your strategy with your rela-

tionships?

3. Reminding people of what they owe you is hard. Why is that?

4. When someone owes you, and they don't seem to be aware that they owe you, how hard is it to keep "anger" out of the conversation?

5. When is not reminding people of what they owe you the right thing to?

6. What debt do you have, and how are you dealing with it?

7. Whom do you owe, and what do you owe them?

8. Is it possible to owe someone who also owes you?

STEP THREE: Commitment - Do it!
4. Expect the best.

Philemon 1:20 & 21
I do wish, brother, that I may have some benefit from you in the Lord; refresh my heart in Christ. Confident of your obedience, I write to you, knowing that you

Why don't we expect the best in any given situation?

Let's admit it. We tend to assume the worst; well, maybe not the worst, but certainly not the best.

Why don't we expect the best? Because expecting the best of people has been a recipe for disappointment. We have expected the best but the kids don't do what they are told. The employees don't do that little extra that makes all the difference. The wife or the husband forgets to do what was promised, takes the other for granted, and makes excuses for not living up to the optimistic vows made on the wedding day.

So expecting the best often leads to disappointment. But if we expect the worst, we will get the worst.

It seems we are stuck in the middle.

Apparently this is more complicated than we tend to think.

Let's look at some real-life situations.

You are the coach of a soccer team. If you do not expect the kids you coach to work hard, listen and obey, and be team players, you probably won't get kids who work hard, listen, follow, and be team players. But just expecting it doesn't make it happen either.

Expectations alone do not make things happen. You need expectations plus a positive relationship.

If you hope to succeed as a coach, you need expectations plus a positive relationship with the kids you are coaching. A relationship that is built on trust which grows little by little as you and the team progress toward desired goals.

Another example: I, as a Pastor, cannot get everyone to do their share of the work that needs to be done at church by just expecting that every member will do it. I must also do the hard work of building people up by encouraging, challenging, rewarding, and caring for them.

Paul has obviously developed a relationship

> will do even more than I ask.

with Philemon, and now he boldly and positively communicates his expectations.

Okay, sounds good, but how does this actually work?

Let's say you are a parent, and you ask your child to clean up his room or clean the garage. And though you had low expectations in the past, this time, you psyched yourself up, and you believe it is going to go well.

Your child starts to clean up but is soon distracted by some newly found, long-forgotten toy. So you get on his case, and he slowly gets back to it. You go through this discouraging routine a few more times, and in frustration and disappointment, you give up on each other.

What went wrong? You had high expectations. You have a life-long relationship with each other. You care about each other. You want the best for each other.

Again you need to understand that having great expectations is not enough. What must you do?

Try to see it as a game. Does your child know the rules of the match? What is winning? What is losing? What do you win if you win? What do you lose if you lose? Is there a right way and a wrong way? What is the reward for the right way? What is the penalty for the wrong way? What is the point of this game anyway? Why is it important? How does this game benefit both of you?

Do you see? You can have high expectations for a clean room or garage, but unless there is a whole support system that both parties have bought into, expectations will only lead to disappointments.

Notice again the step of expecting the best comes at the end of Paul's letter to Philemon. It comes only after a lot of relationship building.

I hope this is making sense to you now. Most relationship problem-solving strategies will only work if there has been a lot of relationship building. Everyone wants to find an easy, simple, cheap, magic technique that will somehow fix relationship problems without going through the time-consuming and hard work of, little by little, building up the relationship.

There is one more crucial secret to Paul's positive expectation of Philemon.

Paul knew that Philemon had given his life to Christ. And there are some things we can assume of those who have given their life to Christ.

They get a new heart. A heart that seeks to love and to sacrifice for the sake of others.

They get a new Spirit. A Spirit of God that seeks to change them into powerful ambassadors of the cause of Christ.

So why not expect the best of someone with a new heart and a new Spirit?

Questions:

1. *Philemon 1:21 Confident of your obedience, I write to you, knowing that you will do even more than I ask.*

   Paul is pretty sure of Philemon's co-operation. Why was Paul so confident?

2. What role does having a good relationship with someone have in expecting the best of them?

3. What best do you expect from your spouse, your children, your parents, your teachers, you bosses, your co-workers, your friends, your pastor, etc.?

4. *Philippians 1:3-6 I thank my God every time I remember you. In all my prayers for all of you, I always pray with joy because of your partnership in the gospel from the first day until now, being confident of this, that he who began a good work in you will carry it on to completion until the day of Christ Jesus.*

   What was the source of Paul's confidence in people?

5. *2 Timothy 1:6-7 For this reason, I remind you to fan into flame the gift of*

God, which is in you through the laying on of my hands. For the Spirit God gave us does not make us timid, but gives us power, love and self-discipline.

What is the source of your confidence in people?

STEP THREE: Commitment - Do it!

5. Ask for a lesser commitment you know they will succeed at.

I live on a lake in the state of Michigan and the ice just melted off it about a month ago. That means the first swim of the new year is just around the corner. I love water, but I don't like the initial getting in. By mid-summer, I just jump in with one plunge. But in the spring, I inch in.

That is what Paul is doing here with Philemon. He is inching into the water. Paul wants something from Philemon. And for the first 21 verses Paul only hints at what he wants.

Hint One: Paul would love it if Philemon

Philemon 1:22 And one thing more: Prepare a guest room for me, because I hope to be restored to you in answer to your prayers.

would allow Onesimus to stay and serve Paul in his hour of need while under house arrest.

Hint Two: Paul would be pleased if Philemon would forgive Onesimus for running away.

Hint Three: Paul would be happy if Philemon would treat Onesimus, not as a slave, but as a brother in Christ.

Finally, in verse 22, Paul makes a straightforward ask - that Philemon would allow Paul to stay at his house if and when Paul ever got to Colossi.

That's it? The big ask is for free lodging?

Asking is hard for most people. It's hard for a few reasons.

One, asking puts the asker in the "I am needy" chair. We like to be self-reliant.

Two, if the request is granted, then there is a debt owed. We have already talked about how most people hate to be in debt.

Three, asking puts the person being asked in a possibly uncomfortable bind. If the person being asked does not want to say yes to the request, they may squirm and try to come up with excuses to say no. All of this is very uncomfortable.

Four, the asker has no idea if the one being asked will say yes or no. That uncertainty is enough to make many people not bother asking.

Five, the ask may be turned down, and who likes the sense of rejection.

Step Three: Commitment - Do it!

And finally, six, if the ask is turned down, how does that affect the relationship? Should both parties involved pretend this never happened? Do they get mad and say something? Does the asker quietly vow never to help this person out if ever there is an opportunity? Do they forgive and forget?

So there is a lot at stake when you ask somebody for something.

Now, as you are thinking about this, what might make the ask easier to do? By now I hope you can guess it.

The ask is infinitely easier the better the relationship. If I ask my brother if I can camp out at his house for a day or two, I can do so with no anxiety whatsoever. I have a positive, long history with him. I know what the answer will be.

But what if I ask to borrow $50,000 from him? Well, I'm not sure about this one. I don't know if he has the money or what such a commitment would do to his plans or what his wife would think. So is there a better place to start than asking for $50,000 from him?

How about a lesser commitment?

It might go something like this. "Hey, I need to borrow $50,000 (for some particular reason), and I am not sure what you could do, but could you, at least, do $1,000?"

See I know he can do $1,000 and would do so without thinking about it. So I am starting with an ask I know he can do. But I have hinted at what I want, haven't I?

He will think about it. He will see what he can do. I will have successfully motivated him to give me all the consideration that he can. He will want to do his best for me.

Now, if in the end he only gives me $1,000, I will be satisfied. Is this all I was hoping for from him? No. But it is enough to keep a positive relationship building. But maybe he can help with more. He will try to do all he can for me.

Why does this work? Let's think about this. The one asking has been dealing with a problem for an extended period. He or she has thought of and discarded many possible solutions. Finally, a real solution is thought of which involves an ask. The asker thinks about how he might ask. He prays about how he might ask. He rehearses the ask. And finally, he delivers the ask.

The one being asked has not been struggling with this problem, and perhaps knows nothing about it. The asker shows up on the doorstep of the one being asked and just blurts out the problem. The one being asked has not been thinking about the asker's problem. He or she has not had time to think about this problem.

People need time to understand a problem that has just presented itself. They need time to decide on whether or not they want to adopt the newly presented problem as their problem (in effect, when you ask something of someone you are giving them your problem).

They will want to think about all the possible solutions. And they will need to come to the same conclusion that the asker did regarding the solution.

So the strategy that Paul employs with Philemon is to make a small ask that buys the time that the one being asked will need to consider in order to make a larger commitment.

Okay, doesn't this sound like manipulation? Maybe. But manipulation is a word we attach to underhanded behavior that tricks or forces people to do what they wouldn't otherwise do.

Paul is not trying to trick Philemon. He is trying to be respectful of the process that is needed for someone to do something they have not had time to think about.

Questions:

1. *Philemon 1:22 And one thing more: Prepare a guest room for me, because I hope to be restored to you in answer to your prayers.*

   Not only does Paul expect the best regarding the whole "Onesimus" question, but he also is not shy about asking for a particular favor. On what basis could Paul be so bold?

2. Notice he assumes Philemon is praying

for him, and Paul lets Philemon know that he, Paul, understands this. Do you expect the people in your life to pray for you?

3. How might you remind them of this expectation?

4. Paul asks specifically here for something that he knows Philemon can easily do. How does asking for a little thing help in the asking of a big thing?

5. Can you think of a time you did this?

6. Can you think of an ask that you are reluctant to make? Why are you unwilling to make this ask?

7. If you were able to think of an ask that you are reluctant to make, can you think of a lesser ask that would take away your reluctance?

STEP THREE: Commitment - Do it!

6. End your conversation talking about you common relationship web.

> Philemon 1:23-25
> Epaphras, my fellow prisoner in Christ Jesus, sends you greetings. And so do Mark, Aristarchus, Demas and Luke, my fellow workers. The grace of the Lord Jesus

Paul begins his letter to Philemon talking about all the people connected to Paul in Philemon's location. He ends his letter talking about all the people related to Philemon in Paul's area.

Epaphras, the first person mentioned here at the end of Paul's letter, is the one who planted the church in Colossi, and he is probably the one who led Philemon to the Lord. We don't know much about the others listed.

Why does Paul mention these people? What do they have to do with the situation? After all, this is an issue between Paul, Philemon, and Onesimus.

A husband and wife have issues with one another. They decide they do not love each other anymore and want to get a divorce. So now they have to tell their eight-year-old son and their ten-year-old daughter. They sit down with their kids and say something like this:

"Mommy and Daddy do not love each other anymore and have decided that it would be better for everyone if we were to separate and live in different houses. This has nothing to do with you. It is just a problem that daddies and mommies sometimes have. And just because we do not love each other anymore, doesn't mean we don't love you. We love you. We will always love you no matter what."

You see the problem with this logic, don't you? If I were one of the kids I would, if I had the courage, respond like this:

"Mom and Dad, how can we believe you when you say that you will always love us no matter what? You both once said these same words to each other. But now you tell us that your love is gone. Where did it go? Why did it end? How can a love that is supposed to be forever, no matter what, end? And then why should we believe you when you say your love for us will never change, no matter what?"

The mistake these two parents are making is to think that their problem with each other is just their problem.

A problem between two people is never just

Christ be with your spirit.

between two people.

Let's say there is one member of your work team that is always complaining about the other team members. If someone makes a mistake, she makes sure everyone else knows about it. And when she is talking about others in a negative manner, there is some truth to what she says, and it is hard not to enjoy hearing it. After all, she is talking about someone else. Of course, when you find out she has been talking negatively about you, that is another story.

This goes on for some time, and soon the whole team is upset, not just with this one person, but everyone is sort of down on everyone. One bad apple can spoil the barrel.

We are connected. Any relationship issue you may have with one person is not just with that one person.

The boss has a hard talk with an employee. The employee goes home and talks about it with his or her spouse. If a layoff is in view, it affects the whole family.

We often naively think that relationship issues are limited to the two that are involved in the fight. Thus the saying, "It takes two to have a fight." And it is true that conflict often erupts between two people - a husband and a wife, a pastor and a member, a boss and an employee, a friend and a friend - but the cause of the conflict and the effect of that conflict is often shared by all kinds of people behind the scenes.

So Paul has a relationship issue with Philemon because Philemon owns the runaway slave Onesimus, and Paul has set him free in the Lord. But the solution to this conflict is not just between them. There is the church that meets in the home of Philemon. There is the group that meets in Rome with Paul. All of this is connected to a worldwide, world-changing movement called Christianity where "all have sinned and fall short of the glory of God." Where there "is neither slave nor free."

What Philemon does or does not do will have repercussions in the grand enterprise.

So Paul ends his letter to Philemon talking about relationships. If you recall, this is how the letter began as well. This should not come to you as a surprise.

Reading between the lines of Paul's letter, I imagine him saying something like this:

Philemon, I am a prisoner of Christ just as Onesimus is your prisoner. By the way, you are a prisoner as well. And we all are part of a big team of people. Some of that team is with you and the church plant that meets in your home. Some of the team is with me in Rome. And as a team, Philemon, what are we trying to do? Tell people about the grace of the Lord Jesus - a grace that grants us unmerited favor - the kind you need to give to your former slave Onesimus. This may be troubling for you, and you may lose some sleep over this, but, in the end, the Lord Jesus will guide you by His Spirit.

Questions:

1. *Philemon 1:23-24 Epaphras, my fellow prisoner in Christ Jesus, sends you greetings. And so do Mark, Aristarchus, Demas and Luke, my fellow workers. The grace of the Lord Jesus Christ be with your spirit.*

   When dealing with a difficult issue with your spouse, your friend, your coworker, your neighbor, or your fellow church member, why is the relationship the topic with which you need to start and end?

2. *Romans 12:5 (LB) We belong to each other and each of us belongs to all the others.*

   1 Corinthians 12:12 Just as a body, though one, has many parts, but all its many parts form one body, so it is with Christ.

   Why is it easy to forget that, though we are many, we are the one body of Christ?

Part Three: The Main Theme of the Book

The issue of slavery

I hope this book/Bible study has helped you rethink, refocus, and perhaps even revamp your approach to the important relationships in your life; in other words, it helps you ***deal with friends and tactfully get along with people***.

The approach of this book/Bible study has been that of a case study. We studied together how Paul dealt with his friends and tactfully got along with his people. Specifically, we examined his approach to resolving a relationship problem with Philemon concerning his runaway slave, Onesimus. We broke the problem down into its various parts. Next, we tried to figure out why Paul wrote what he wrote to fix the problem. We then attempted to extract relationship principles from the whole process that Paul went through. And finally, we tried to apply these principles to resolving our relationship problems.

However, when Paul wrote the letter to Philemon, he probably was not just attempting to show us how to deal with friends and more tactfully get along with the people around us.

He wrote the letter because the Philemon/Onesimus problem was an example of a growing clash between Christianity and the rest of the culture of that day in regard to how people were to be treated - especially as it related to the institution of slavery.

How were Christians supposed to deal with the issue of slavery?

If you read what Paul says about slavery in the rest of the Bible, it can be quite confusing.

For example, in 1 Timothy 6:1, Paul seems to tolerate slavery.

> *(NIV) All who are under the yoke of slavery should consider their masters worthy of full respect so that God's name and our teaching may not be slandered.*

Roman law allowed for slavery. Paul could not set slaves free. But many slaves were responding to the gospel - the good news that all men are sinners, all men need to be saved by the cross of Christ, and that all men are to be prized, cherished children of the living God. This was good news to slaves.

This good news did two things. It gave slaves, not only hope that this life could be better, but it also gave them a sense of meaning and purpose that extended into eternity.

But, as often is the case, as the hope for change increased, patience for the change decreased. Slaves, especially newly-come-to-the-Lord slaves, wanted to be treated as brothers and sisters in the Lord.

But if a non-Christian master owned a slave, what could Christians do about it?

Paul goes on to say in 1 Timothy 6:2-3 (NIV):

> *Those (slaves) who have believing masters should not show them disrespect just because they are fellow believers. Instead, they should serve them even better because their masters are dear to them as fellow believers and are devoted to the welfare of their slaves.*

Okay, you can sense the growing tension, especially when both the master and the slave become Christians.

As is almost always the case, the party that is suffering sees the implication of the new hope in Christ before those that are doing well - i.e. the Christian slaves see the consequences of the gospel in terms of their status before the Christian masters do. And we probably can infer from these two verses that some of the Christian slaves were starting to press their cause.

So Paul reminds the slaves that, though they

may be in the right, they still must show respect to their Christian masters.

And I think Paul, in the end, is saying that the Christian masters are in the wrong though he doesn't come right out and say this.

Why do I think this way? Listen to what Paul says to Philemon.

> *Philemon 1:15-16 Maybe this is the reason that Onesimus was separated from you (Philemon) for a while so that you might have him back forever-- no longer as a slave but more than a slave--that is, as a dearly loved brother. He is especially a dearly loved brother to me. How much more can he become a brother to you, personally and spiritually in the Lord!*

Paul seems pretty explicit here. Well, sort of. He does qualify his statement a little by starting with the word, "Maybe."

There are other passages where Paul is challenging the status quo of ranking some people as less and some people as more important based on status, race, religion, and gender.

> *Colossians 3:1-3,11 Since, then, you have been raised with Christ, set your hearts on things above, where Christ is, seated at the right hand of God. 2 Set your minds on things above, not on earthly things. 3 For you died, and your life is now hidden with Christ in God.... 11 Here there is no Gentile or Jew, circumcised or uncircumcised, barbarian, Scythian,*

> slave or free, but Christ is all, and is in all.
>
> Galatians 3:26-28 So in Christ Jesus you are all children of God through faith, for all of you who were baptized into Christ have clothed yourselves with Christ. There is neither Jew nor Gentile, neither slave nor free, nor is there male and female, for you are all one in Christ Jesus.

At first glance, these two passages seem to eliminate slavery completely. But if slavery is being eliminated, so is freedom, not to mention male and female.

So what is Paul trying to say?

At the very least, I think he is saying that the status identifiers of that day, like male and female, Jew and Greek, and slave and free do not count in the Christian world. They still may exist, but none of them make you more or less valuable, more or less necessary, more or less loved, or more or less Christian.

So what do you think Paul is ultimately doing?

I think Paul has a gospel strategy to change the culture, and I think it is a strategy that we can learn from today.

Let me tell you a story.

My brother, Jim, and my friend, Henry Reyenga (who happens to be the president of Christian Leaders Institute), and I had just finished a round of golf. It was the first time my brother and Henry had met. Henry learned in our round of golf that Jim and his wife were not, as of then, able to have children.

Henry's phone rang. It was the Pastor whom Henry had mentored into pastoring a church Henry had planted in Oregon. This pastor had a problem. There was a young girl that had just started coming to his church, a girl in trouble. She made a living in the strip bars. She got pregnant. She had thought about abortion, but having started going to the church, figured out that life was sacred. She wanted to find a good Christian home for her baby, and so this young pastor was calling Henry, his mentor, to ask if he knew of a good Christian home for this unborn child.

It has been 17 years since that day, and my brother and sister-in-law have a delightful, beautiful, God-loving daughter.

Why? Because there was a church and a pastor that chose not to condemn a young mother who had all kinds of sin in her life. The pastor and his church instead strategically did three things: One, they loved her with the love of God, a love demonstrated by the sacrifice of Jesus Christ on the cross. Two, they got her into a habit of reading the Word of God. Three, they gave her and the Holy Spirit time to work the love and the Word of God into her life.

Historically, this is what Christianity has done all over the world for the last 2,000 years. Christians would share Christ in some part of the world that was without Christ and His Church, and gradually the culture would be transformed into the image of Christ and His Church.

This seems to be Paul's strategy with Philemon, with the broader Christian community, and with the pagan culture around him.

He preached the need for Christ for all people. He preached freedom through Christ for all people who wanted it. He preached the gifts of the Spirit given to all who believe in Christ. And finally, he preached the truth that all who gave their lives to Christ and His Church were brothers and sisters in the Lord, without regard to status, wealth, gender, race, or country.

The end result of this strategy? Slavery, as an institution, would disappear.

Paul makes one more argument - a more philosophical argument. One that turns words like "slavery" and "freedom" on their heads.

> *1 Corinthians 7:21-23 Were you a slave when you were called? Don't let it trouble you--although if you can gain your freedom, do so. For the one who was a slave when called to faith in the Lord is the Lord's freed person; similarly, the one who was free when called is Christ's slave. You were bought at a price; do not become slaves of human beings.*

According to these verses Paul seems to be saying that though, according to Roman law a person might be a slave, that same person might at the same time be free according to

God's way of thinking. And conversely, though you may be free according to Roman law, you might be slave according to God's way of thinking.

How does this work?

Slavery and freedom in the big picture are about your status with God and His Kingdom, not about your relationship to the government of the day. Slavery and freedom come down to a choice between two options.

Option One: If you freely choose to follow Christ, you become a slave to Him and you reap the reward for your slavery to Him - that is freedom from the grip of sin and death.

Options Two: If you freely chose to follow anything else, you become a slave to whatever it is that you are following, and you then reap the reward of that slavery.

> 2 Peter 2:19 (NIV) They promise them freedom, while they themselves are slaves of depravity—for "people are slaves to whatever has mastered them."

Freedom is not a state of being. Freedom is only a choice between one master or another.

So why not choose a master who has your best interest at heart?

Endnotes and Questions:

It has been a privilege to lead you through this amazing book of the Bible. What it lacks in volume, it makes up for with incredible principles that apply to the issues we deal with in everyday life.

I hope this study has lived up to the title, *How to Influence Friends and Tactfully Get Along with People.*

The following questions are here to help you think about the book as a whole. They are optional. You can skip them. You can answer them for yourself. Or you can schedule one more meeting for your small group.

1. Which one of the relationship principles in this book was new to you? Why?

2. Which one of the relationship principles in this book do you struggle to apply to your life the most? Why?

3. Before reading this book, which of the relationship principles found in this book did you ignore or violate the most in dealing with friends and influencing people? Why?

4. After reading this book, which of the relationship principles found in this book will you try to apply to your relationships the most? Why?

5. Which verse in the book of Philemon do you still not quite understand?

6. How has this study made a difference in your marriage, in your family, with your friendships, among your workmates or your schoolmates or your churchmates?

7. If you happened to do this study with a small group, how has this study changed how people treat each other in the Bible study group itself?

Notes

Made in United States
Troutdale, OR
02/24/2024

17894408R00090